PAINTING THE JOY OF THE SOUL

P Buckley Moss®

by Peter Rippe

LANDAUER BOOKS
Landauer Corporation
Cumming, Iowa

PAINTING THE JOY OF THE SOUL—P. BUCKLEY MOSS
Art Copyright 1997 by P. Buckley Moss
Text Copyright 1997 by P. Buckley Moss Galleries, Ltd.

Published by:
Landauer Books
A division of Landauer Corporation
12251 Maffitt Road, Cumming, Iowa 50061

President and Publisher: Jeramy Lanigan Landauer
Editor: Becky Johnston
Art Director: Lyne Neymeyer
Copy Editor: Joanna Heist
Copy Reviewing Editor: Linda Delbridge-Parker
Layout Production: Nicole Bratt

Library of Congress Cataloging-in-Publication Data
Rippe, Peter, 1937-
      P. Buckley Moss: Painting the Joy of the Soul / by Peter Rippe.
          p.   cm.
      Includes index.
      ISBN 0-09-648709-7(hc)
      1. Moss, P. Buckley (Pat Buckley), 1933-   . 2. Artists—United States—Biography. I. Moss, P. Buckley (Pat Buckley), 1933-   .
II. Title. III. Title: P. Buckley Moss : Painting the Joy of the Soul.
N6537.M669R56 1997
760'.092
[B]—DC21   97-6728
                                                                          CIP
ISBN 0-964870-9-7

This book is printed on acid-free paper.
Printed in Hong Kong.

10 9 8 7 6 5 4 3 2 1

I am sometimes asked why I don't paint the reality of violence and starvation. It is because I am dedicated to painting not the tragedy of the moment, but the hope of the future—hopes that will seed positive thoughts of love, family, and the beauty of our world.

WINTER VISITOR, Offset print,
Image size: 23½" x 12⅞", 1974/78
An early limited edition print made
from a now lost original watercolor
painting.

This is one of the pieces that firmly
established the Valley Style of
P. Buckley Moss in the minds and
hearts of her collectors.

A lone goose stands front and
center. Behind the goose at least
thirty horizon lines fade off into the
background, past trees and bushes
and a distant Shenandoah bank
barn. This work of mood and
memory conjures up images of
nature as well as moods of
temperament. The work of art is
realistic, modernistic, abstract, and
non-objective all at the same time.

FOREWORD: A MEMOIR

Several years ago, I was invited by the International Association for the Visual Arts to curate an exhibition of paintings by P. Buckley Moss. This collection would be the keynote for one of the largest arts and crafts festivals in the Southwest: Kermezaar. My research into the artist's life and work impressed upon me her faith in the power of creativity, the appeal of the familiar, and the pursuit of hope and goodness as artistic themes. Later, when I actually began the installation of her paintings, I felt the full impact of her visual achievements as well as the gifted persona behind the tableaux. On one level, I could not help but admire a beguiling naiveté of composition, while on another, a form of subtle symbolism like a poetic line by Frost, simple and also complex!

Of course the exhibition was a great success attended by thousands. The personal appearances made by our guest artist enriched the lives of children who still need hope, but came away from her art class demonstrations especially exalted. As one teacher of art observed, "If we could only have a role model like P. Buckley Moss for every class and subject!"

At the special dinner given to honor P. Buckley Moss prior to her departure, we lamented the imminent return of her exhibition to Waynesboro and the artist's leaving as well. Her paintings and her conversations had touched us all and we were better for those experiences. Alas, only the remembrance remains.

Thankfully, such is no longer the case or the problem, for in his scholarly biography and catalogue, "Painting the Joy of the Soul—P. Buckley Moss," Peter Rippe accurately, incisively, and passionately has captured the kaleidoscopic essence of America's most popular living woman artist. In his text and by her art, P. Buckley Moss will always live.

Leonard P. Sipiora

Leonard P. Sipiora
Former Director, El Paso Museum of Art;
President, Leonard Sipiora Fine Art & Antiques

INTRODUCTION

Patricia Providence Elizabeth Buckley Moss Henderson—
a name suggesting the complexities and the interests
of the owner's life: Patricia for St. Patrick of Ireland, a
favorite saint of her much-beloved and very Irish paternal
grandfather; Providence in remembrance of her Italian
maternal grandmother who perished in the tragic New
York Triangle Shirtways Factory fire; Elizabeth, a "new"
second name adopted during the artist's Cooper Union
years probably in honor of her remarkable mother;
Buckley, her maiden name proudly reflecting an Irish-
American Catholic heritage; Moss for her first husband
Jack, their six children, and her professional image; and
Henderson for Malcolm, her second husband and business
manager, and for the popular acclaim and success that have
come to her as "The People's Artist," P. Buckley Moss.

 Complexity as well as simplicity form the natural
and the paradoxical sides of Pat Moss' artistic persona.

A very prolific artist, she regularly creates hundreds of new
images every year. Moss is fully capable of painting an
assortment of impressive watercolors quickly and easily,
and she usually has at least several such works in progress
at the same time. A few words from a friend or admirer, an
advertisement in a newspaper or magazine, or a
photograph provided by proud parents or a would-be
collector easily inspire her to create a series of new works,
all reassuringly similar in overall style and composition yet,
at the same time, each one uniquely different in color
emphasis, focal point, and play of lines.

Along with her bounteous spirit of invention, Moss goes
through phases when she returns time and again to old
familiar—and immensely popular—themes such as
Amish/Mennonites, geese, trees, and winter reflections.

 Still, out of what has become an impressive
production, surfaces a select group of amazing

masterpieces that deftly combine the directness of her nearly trademarked brand of abstract expressionism with the mystical convolutions of a Medieval icon.

While some critics have charged that the works of P. Buckley Moss are simple—even, they say, too simple to be considered art—the masses of the general public love her work, finding joy in almost everything she creates. Again on the negative side, Moss has been called a popular illustrator whose drawings at best belong only on greeting cards and souvenir items.

Still, museums have given her exhibits and some scholars, especially those from the disciplines of philosophy and theology, have found her work to have profound meaning and prophetic vision.

Moss has the professional reputation of a paradox, an artist who embraces publicity and public acclaim while seemingly shunning the inner circles of the art world.

None of this seems to bother Pat Moss. She creates not as an enigma from behind the scenes, but proudly and publicly as somebody who knows what she wants to say and who has the power to say it loudly and clearly. And the people hear—as they seriously collect the wisdom and art of P. Buckley Moss.

Peter M. Rippe, Director

P. Buckley Moss Museum

Photography: Dave Morrison

I am sixty-four years old and, as I look back on my life, I see that, apart from my very early years and the ten years of having babies, my commitment to painting and drawing has been paramount in every aspect of my life.

Even in those early years, I drew while my siblings read. The written word was unintelligible to me. When asked to read the word "cat," I would say "kitty" because the letters meant nothing and I could only guess at words by association with the pictures in a book or with the story.

Very early on, art became my refuge and consolation. Later, when all else spelled failure in school, it became my one point of recognition and praise.

When marriage and the six babies came in rapid succession, I still found time each day to create at least one small painting or drawing. Even now, if a day goes by on which I am denied the opportunity to create, it is a sad one for me. Painting is my meditation, and without it I am thrown off balance.

I believe that what I have said in these few words explains why I am a compulsive painter and how my being dyslexic led me to communicate through my art. I am one with my art. It is who I am and this book is my life, both in substance and in spirit. It is yours to read and judge. I can be no other than what you find here.

P. Buckley Moss

A COMMUNITY SPIRIT, Watercolor, 18" x 24", 1996
This Amish barn-raising piece was painted as the original for an edition of 2,000 offset prints, 1,000 of which were given to the Mennonite Central Committee for fundraising purposes.

The painting depicts a traditional Amish barn-raising possibly based on a similar scene witnessed by the artist in Lancaster County, Pennsylvania. To add to the early American feeling of the painting, Pat has segmented the work as if it were a wall stencil with a circular center and four surrounding corner patterns—parts of a pattern that together create a whole work.

The importance of a strong work ethic is a significant part of Pat Moss' philosophy. This painting depicts the work ethic in the life of a vital Amish community as its members join together to create a viable farm structure for one family that will with time strengthen the economic, religious, and political life of the whole community.

Like the over-riding stencil pattern of this painting, the piece pays tribute to individuals, the parts, who will work together for the good of the community, the whole.

TABLE OF CONTENTS

CHAPTER ONE
Early Influences

The Flawed Muse P. Buckley Moss was born on May 20, 1933, in the Richmond Borough of New York City. She was the second of three children, two girls and a boy, born to Vincent William Buckley and Elizabeth Panno Buckley.

During the first few months of Pat's life, the family resided with her paternal grandparents in a home located at 3855 Amboy Road in Great Kills on New York's Staten Island.

When Pat was about ten months old, Vincent and Elizabeth moved their growing family into their own home at 3843 Amboy Road, which would become Pat's childhood home.

Of Sicilian-Italian ancestry on her mother's side and Irish-American ancestry from her father's family, young Patricia Buckley was brought up within the apparently conservative structure of a firmly middle-class Catholic American family.

While old family photographs show the Buckleys and their friends living what appears to be the typical family life of the 1930's, strong hints of dysfunctional undercurrents appear in the historical records.

Much later in her life, after becoming a very successful artist, Pat Moss wrote about being "depressed about the atmosphere at home...My father was invariably drunk by the end of the day; my mother screamed at him and he shouted back. It was very sad."

Despite her nagging sense of melancholy relative to her father, Pat also notes that "He was one of the kindest men you could ever meet. He was everybody's friend and never spoke ill of anyone. His belief in the good in people eventually proved to be his undoing when business associates took advantage of this natural trust. This led him to alcoholism and heavy smoking. He died at the age of 64. I still mourn his loss, not just for myself but also for my children whose experience of this gentle dignified man was tragically cut short."

There is no doubt that Pat's father was an alcoholic and that her mother protected him and his reputation, perhaps at times even at the expense of her own career and professional advancement.

Still, amid the stress of parental difficulties and divided attentions, the future artist of family values developed a relationship with her mother that remains to this day at the cutting edge of the P. Buckley Moss persona.

Elizabeth ("Letizia"—her original Italian name with the spelling she prefers) Panno Buckley, the artist's mother, was and remains even at ninety-three a strong and determined woman. Born in Sicily on

February 9, 1904, she arrived in New York City with her family in 1907. Her mother Providencia (the Italian spelling was Provvidenza) had been contracted into a loveless marriage at a very young age. Elizabeth was the last of ten children to be born to this union. Elizabeth's father, Francesco Panno, was considerably older than her mother.

In March of 1911 when Elizabeth was only seven years old, her mother perished in a fire while working as a low-wage seamstress in the infamous New York Triangle Shirtways Factory. She was one of 146 people who died in the terrible fire—most were seamstresses who had reportedly been locked in the building. According to family history, Providencia was trying to earn enough money to return her family to Italy, a goal that she would have realized in June of 1911, three months after the tragic fire.

About three years after the death of his wife, Francesco returned to Sicily where he married again. The fact that he'd taken a new wife, the principal of a boarding school in his old hometown, did not set well with his children back in New York City.

Later while trying to reclaim some of his former property, he was murdered under questionable circumstances.

Pat's mother, Elizabeth, was seventeen at the time and under the direct care of an older brother and several other siblings. These events in her own life appear to have convinced this young obviously attractive Italian girl that life was hard and that if she wanted to make a success of her own life, she would have to use her personality, her wit, and her intelligence to surmount her immigrant circumstances.

Fortunately, a remarkable school in downtown New York City specialized in the practical training of young women whose foreign background and ethnic roots were apt to be viewed with suspicion and prejudice. The Washington Irving School for Girls in the heart of Manhattan had been founded to specifically imbue its students (often immigrant) with the American work ethic. There, Elizabeth Panno learned a trade—clothing design—and in time she became a successful designer of children's clothing, actually working in the same garment district where her mother had perished years before.

As Pat tells the story, "My mother saw an advertisement in the New York Times for an assistant designer in a fashion house. She applied for the job saying she had been assistant designer at Jack Borgenichts & Company. This was a risky thing to do because she had never worked for the company, though her sister Angie had previously, and she had visited Angie at Borgenichts on a couple of occasions. Anyhow, she got the job and started on a career that would eventually take her to be the chief designer for the Catton Brothers who specialized in children's clothing.

"My mother has a natural artistic sense. Before her marriage, she had a job painting floral designs onto dresses. She would copy the design from reproductions of floral paintings found in books. Much of my success as an artist I attribute to my mother. From her came both encouragement and a sense of design. She is a lady imbued with indomitable spirit and her example has carried me through the difficult passages in my life."

At the age of twenty-six, Elizabeth eloped with Vincent Buckley, a handsome young man from a solid New York City Irish-American family. They were married in a civil ceremony on March 25, 1929, without the knowledge of his family. However, her brothers and sisters and other family members were aware of and pleased with the match.

ELIZABETH PANNO AND VINCENT BUCKLEY, Photograph, 1929
Elizabeth Panno and Vincent Buckley between March and June, 1929.

"Liz" and "Buck" were legally married at the time, but not living together. Elizabeth was staying at a friend's home waiting for Vincent to tell his family and for the official nuptials in a Catholic church.

Pat recalls, "My mother tells me that when she and my father were married, they had five dollars between them. My father came from an Irish family, his father having started work at the age of eight as a mule driver on the Erie Canal. Through the determination and natural wit of my grandfather, the family had prospered, and by the time of my father's marriage, it was a respected middle-class Irish family living on Staten Island.

"Instead of choosing himself an Irish bride, my father had fallen in love with a lively and beautiful Sicilian girl. Arriving after the Irish, the Italians (the newest immigrants) were at the bottom of the social ladder. The marriage was far from popular."

Only after the kind intervention of one of Vincent's uncles who had independently learned about the marriage did his parents hear of their new Italian daughter-in-law.

THE QUEEN BEE, Oil on artist's board, 23" x 17", 1966/74
Portrait of the artist's mother—also called "My Mother."

Elizabeth Buckley is shown as a beautiful woman in her mid- to late-60's. The work has gone through several over-paintings to achieve its highly sophisticated mood. While purple is one of the artist's favorite colors, Elizabeth says she favors blue. In this piece, the blue and the purple blend to create a feeling of attentive awareness. Notice how the light seems to emanate from the subject's face and hair.

"Grandpa Buckley," Elizabeth says, "accepted her with a hug and invited the young couple to come live with them in the Buckley home on Staten Island." She notes, however, that "Grandma Buckley was never happy with the situation and predicted that Vincent would have to eat spaghetti for the rest of his life."

In June, 1929, four months after their civil wedding, Vincent and Elizabeth renewed their marriage vows in a Roman Catholic Church. This official blessing was required by both sides of their respectively Catholic families.

Four years later Patricia, their second daughter, was born and the Vincent Buckley family had a home of their own across a field from the senior Buckleys. Later, Elizabeth used some of her savings to buy a cottage on the Delaware River in Mill Rift, Pennsylvania, as a summer retreat away from the increasingly unhappy situation developing in the city. Her husband's growing alcoholism was becoming a dominant force in the Buckley family life.

Elizabeth, however, with her indomitable personality and her personal ambitions, would not allow herself to be defeated. Her triumphal spirit, her Catholic faith, and her great sense of humor have served Elizabeth Panno Buckley well over the years. She survived her husband's alcoholism and his long illness and ultimate death from lung cancer.

Today (1997) at the age of ninety-three, "Gran Liz" as she is called, remains a positive force in the lives of almost everyone who comes in contact with her through Pat, the Moss Museum, and the P. Buckley Moss Society.

Despite her mother's forceful and endearing personality, none of her maternal Italian relatives appear to have played much of a role in Pat's early development.

As a child her life was dominated by various Buckley relations and especially by her grandfather, the kindly Daniel J. Buckley.

This openly demonstrative old Irishman, a retired engineer from the Baltimore and Ohio Railroad,

FATHER, Watercolor, 12" x 5¼", 1988 Portrait of the artist's father—also called "My Father."

An elegant and idealized presentation of the artist's father, Vincent Buckley.
Background references relate to Wall Street in New York City where Vincent was a stockbroker.

appropriately nicknamed the young girl "Split-the-Wind" because she seemed to be always running...from her own house to her beloved Grandfather's abode. His exuberant personality remains one of the artist's most cherished memories.

Pat later wrote: "Grandpa Buckley was a considerable influence in my life. From a mule driver, he rose to being an engineer on the Staten Island Rapid Transit. He taught himself to read and took a wide interest in all matters. He became a prominent member of the local theatrical group and such a well-respected citizen that when he died in 1956, the *Staten*

GRANDPA AND
GRANDMA BUCKLEY
Photograph, ca. 1935
The artist's grandmother and grandfather (center) with a friend of Mrs. Buckley (left) and Mary Buckley Cassidy (right) about 1935.

Grandpa Daniel Buckley rallied Pat's self-confidence at a time when it appeared to her that everybody else thought she was a failure.

Throughout the artist's childhood, this kindly Irish-American gentleman remained a rock of love and inspiration for Pat.

Island Advance published a long feature article about his life.

"It was Grandpa who gave me the name 'Split-the-Wind.' Whenever there was a message to be taken from our house to his, I would be the one to volunteer. I'd run like crazy across the field knowing he would probably be watching, and every time I'd try to get there faster than before.

"My memories are of him sitting in his brown rocker in the bay window waiting for me to come back from school. I felt that I was his special favorite; he called me 'Patrick.' My school days were not easy. My grandfather though had a great faith in me and, unlike others, he never let me feel that my problems were of my own making.

"Sitting on the floor beside his rocker, I could talk to him as a real friend. He listened with patience to everything I had to say and never spoke down to me. He made me truly believe that if I wanted to do something and tried my hardest, I would succeed."

Like many other Catholic families of that day and age, Pat Buckley's education began in

GRANDPA, Watercolor, 12⅞" × 10⅛", 1988
Pat's remembrance painting of her grandfather.

Pat painted her beloved grandpa looking much as he does in the previous photograph; he is a thoughtful presence. Notice how the eyes of the old man seem to glance toward the little girl who is obviously Pat herself. Although this is an idealized representation, the relationship so subtly suggested by this painting is just as real because it was an important factor in the artist's actual childhood development.

her local parochial grade school under the strict and guiding tutelage of nuns.

St. Clare's, as Pat wrote in her autobiography, suddenly introduced her young free spirit to the world of reality and discipline. The serious sisters of St. Clare's didn't have much time for a little girl whose mind "was always racing…often, in the realm of fantasy."

Pat describes herself as a dreamer whose world could not be confined to schoolroom subjects, catechism religion, and everyday expectations.

Looking back, Pat says, "I was charged with enormous energy. My mind was always racing and often in the realm of fantasy. I could not confine it.

"When I had explored the limits of reality, I would move into my fantasy world where beauty and adventure and challenges were around every corner.

"I was totally unprepared for the discipline of school; and the reading that I knew would be so easy turned out to be a frustration that I could never overcome.

"Today's educators recognize that many young people suffer a learning disability called dyslexia and, in many cases but alas not in all, constructive help is given to these children. Not so in my young days when at first I was described as inattentive, then a slow learner, and finally stupid. I tried hard to read. I wanted very much to get it right and to bring an end to people laughing at me. I worked hard at learning the words. I almost knew what they were but somehow I always seemed to get it wrong. I began to dread the reading classes.

"Throughout my schooling, I fought this disadvantage. Sometimes the odds would seem too great and I would escape to my own imaginary world of horses, skating, and heroic deeds—a world where a noble spirit counted for more than a learned mind."

Dyslexia and other related learning difficulties were not well understood during the 1930's—a situation that persists at least in part to the present day. If a student didn't respond to her teachers in a way they thought appropriate, they considered her to be stupid, lazy, or at best, a child with an immature attention span that required disciplining.

According to Helene Gruber, a past President of the Association for Children and Adults with Learning Disabilities (ACLD, Inc.), "The term 'learning disabilities' was first defined in 1962 and, although a report to Congress in 1987 revealed that 5 to 10 percent of the American population may have learning disabilities, a general lack of comprehension regarding the condition still exists."

Dr. Gruber, who is personally familiar with this case, has commented that, "Many youngsters today can relate to Pat's early encounter with disappointment. They, too, approached school with unbridled enthusiasm, only to experience failure, diminished self-esteem and, in general, frustration."

She goes on to say that "When examining the lives of successful individuals with learning disabilities, one discovers a common factor: support from a person who believed in their abilities and their worth when all others seemed to have abandoned belief in any potential to succeed. In Pat's case, it was Grandfather Buckley who rallied her self-confidence.

"While today's more enlightened educators recognize that many potentially destructive learning differences need not lead to failure and that there are legitimate alternative ways of human perception that are either tolerable, with understanding and special instructions, or treatable, Patricia Buckley was one of those young people who suffered the consequences of misunderstanding and academic misclassification."

At least in part, school was an unhappy experience for Pat.

Her Pupil's Record from St. Clare's documents A's and B's until she entered the fifth grade which she had to repeat. From that point on, C's dominated. History, geography, spelling, and reading are all listed as problem areas. At the end of her second year in the fifth grade, her teacher wrote that Patricia Buckley was not proficient in anything. A sad but thankfully fallacious verdict for a child whose future ideas and works would delight thousands.

It's hard to determine whether Pat's problem was dyslexia—the inability to learn to read in the

A VISIT TO THE PRINCIPAL'S OFFICE, Watercolor, 11½" x 10½", 1988
Illustrates the artist's feelings about her school days at St. Clare's Catholic School in Great Kills on New York's Staten Island.

While this painting's format is similar to Pat's painting of Grandpa Buckley and herself, its mood is entirely different. The two figures, the nun and the little girl, do not interact whatsoever. The formidable figure of the principal is kindly, but that kindliness doesn't seem to include the little Pat figure who shares no more with the nun than she does with the chair on her left. This is an interesting memory painting for Pat.

absence of any other handicapping condition—or some other problem that the formal school situation exaggerated or could not address.

Upon reflection, Pat summarizes, "The only praise I received was for my drawings. Often I was in trouble because I would be drawing when I should have been doing something else. However, when it was time to draw, I was both my happiest and at my most confident. My drawings followed the paths of my fantasies, creating a world in which I would like to live—a world of harmony where every creature and every plant had the space and freedom to excel.

"Drawing and painting assumed a psychological importance early in my life. I might be a dunce at the written word, but I could tell stories through my drawings. There was seldom a day when I did not do this, and half a century later, I still rue the day in which there is no time for me to draw."

Nonetheless, in all its scenarios, many of the accepted ingredients of a serious education became symbolic dragons for Pat and she began to see herself as a dragon slayer.

Much later in life, the imagery of Pat against the world continues, and she interacts with classes of learning-disabled students and tells them to overcome their feelings of inadequacy and to "do their own thing" to the best of their abilities.

Her experience with the nuns at St. Clare's, who concluded their written academic record of Pat by citing that she was on trial, actually laid the groundwork for an attitude that persisted in Pat's mind, first with all of her future teachers and professors and later toward all art critics in general.

Pat observes, "As I progressed through high school, my learning abilities continued to improve. A problem now lay in a clash of personalities. The head of the school's art department found me to be too strong-willed for her liking.

"Having struggled through those early years, often feeling in a world separate from the others, I suppose I must have developed stubborn individualism. This manifested itself in my art, where I felt confident that it was my right to use my own way of expressing my feelings and emotions."

CHAPTER TWO
Early Inspirations

Ad Majorem Dei Gloriam "AMDG" is the abbreviation of the traditional Jesuit motto St. Clare's Catholic School nuns required all students to write at the head of their papers: "All for the honor and glory of God."

This very Catholic idea of honoring God with one's thoughts and works remains a vital part of the artist's life—she is very much a "visceral Catholic" who says that "all my art is religious."

Although those traditional Jesuit initials are now gone from her work, the AMDG continued to appear on Pat's handwritten documents and in her meticulously written diary notes until well into the 1960's.

This notion of giving all glory to God is a remarkable concept, especially for a little girl whose teachers tended to humiliate her, whose family life was troubled, and whose academic achievements, for one reason or another, seemed to be always on the decline.

While Pat could hardly ever honor God with grades of C's or lower in reading, arithmetic, and history, her perceptive teacher, Sister Regis, discovered one subject in which Pat was indeed exceptional—art. God could be honored.

So it was that after graduation from St. Clare's elementary school in 1947, again with the help of her persistent mother, Pat Buckley was allowed to enter public high school outside of her Staten Island, Richmond Borough.

Naturally, she was enrolled in her mother's alma mater located in midtown Manhattan, the Washington Irving School for Girls.

Pat's academic improvement was noticeable, and her creative abilities increased correspondingly. With the coaching of a few perceptive teachers and the abiding interest of the school's progressive principal, Mary Meade, a sister of well-known anthropologist Margaret Meade, Pat created her first art portfolio. The school's approach, designed to meet the needs of immigrants, somehow fit Pat's academic requisites.

She says, "I know now that this was the turning point in my life. Until then I had struggled to be accepted as an intelligent human being.

"Now my confidence grew and the barriers that existed between me and the academic subjects began to come down. I started to make headway where before I had despaired of ever understanding.

"My accounts of school were now a pleasure to Grandpa. He said, 'I told you you could do it, Patrick. I told you we'd beat them.' For him this was his second success, his first being his own self-taught schooling.

I am very mean.

I am a goat.

My name is Billy,

and

"Billy Mean-Goat" was created by Pat when she was a student at Washington Irving High School. It's the story of a little boy named Daniel (her Grandpa's name) and a rather difficult goat named Billy. The two meet when the little boy happens to invade the goat's territory.

At first, the goat lives up to his name—"Mean-Goat," but in time the two become best friends and the goat introduces Danny to all his forest friends.

This story appears to be autobiographical since Pat and her grandfather certainly shared a similar opinion of school.

The goat represents freedom and an avenue for friendships, both characteristic of the art career that was beginning to appeal to the young but increasingly determined Patricia Buckley.

"The encouragement that he gave to me now motivates my own desire to encourage those who suffer from learning problems."

The young student's creative talents appeared in an interesting artifact from those days, a little story book both "written and illustrated by Patricia Buckley." Through the autobiographical tale of Billy Mean-Goat, Pat presented herself as a little boy with her grandfather's name who meets a somewhat challenging goat, perhaps representing a metaphorical symbol of freedom (from school and other restraints) and spontaneous creativity (the fine arts?).

In Pat's short story, the main character Daniel fishes in what the goat considers to be his stream. "Do you know who I am?" the goat blusters. "No, but my friends call me Danny-Boy!" Later on, the boy and the goat become best of friends, playing together with other forest animals...until Danny-Boy announces that "Tomorrow I have to go back to the city and get ready for school."

Tragedy was averted only when Danny-Boy said that he would come back next summer. It was as if Pat had found her own place in the world—with a free-spirited friend...art? School, winter, and the city kept her away, but not for very long.

Because of Washington Irving's residential requirement, young Patricia was directly exposed to her mother's native Italian culture, probably for the first time in her life.

Because policy required her to live within school district boundaries, Pat stayed with one of her mother's sisters, her Aunt Mary Barretta. At that time, Italian food and Italian culture became important aspects of her life.

One could also conclude that her growing love of the arts—her own Billy Mean-Goat—increased in part in proportion to her growing sense of Italian ethnicity.

During these exciting years, the young artist's world expanded rapidly—intellectually, culturally, and emotionally. Since her mother worked within twenty blocks of her school, Pat could observe Elizabeth Buckley's explosive creativity first-hand.

As Pat later wrote, "Mother was a particular influence at this time. She was working in midtown Manhattan and on those evenings when I didn't have late projects to attend to at school, I would take the subway from 14th Street to 34th Street and walk through Macy's to her 'office,' a small room where she did her designing and cutting of patterns. There I would wait, watching her at her work."

Pat's interest in her mother's work is reflected in two fashion drawings she completed in 1950. They are entirely derivative pieces, quite outside Pat's own style and area of interest. They do, however, demonstrate quite clearly the daughter's admiration for and desire to emulate the mother.

Pat's artistic talent and her cultural and religious interests expanded enormously in the milieu of a big-city environment. Still, records show that the young student continued to be a trial for some of her teachers, especially those with whom her independent personality clashed.

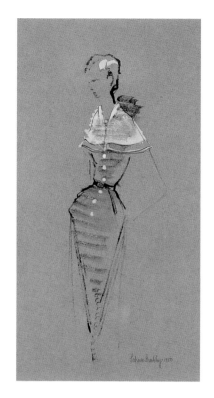

FASHION PIECE ONE,
Ink and white pastel,
13" x 6½", 1950
Fashion Piece One.

This piece was drawn while Pat was a student at Washington Irving High School in Manhattan. Pat's mother designed children's clothing, and she often visited her mother's "office" in New York City's famous Garment District.

FASHION PIECE TWO,
Ink and white pastel,
16" x 8", 1950
Fashion Piece Two.

Pat attributes her great sense of design to her mother.

Even in something as defined and derivative as a fashion drawing, Pat demonstrates an acute awareness of balance and composition.

Notice how Pat directs the viewer's eye from the white glove on the skirt to the neckline and then to the second glove. This is fashion quickly becoming art.

This ongoing problem recurred when the head of Washington Irving's art department submitted to the principal a list of those who might be eligible for art scholarships. Pat Buckley's name was missing.

Again, as at St. Clare's, a teacher's judgement could have been critical. Mary Meade, however, sent this potentially damaging list back to her department with a query: "Where was the name of the talented student whose art seemed to say so much…?"

Patricia Buckley received a college scholarship to the Cooper Union in New York City, one of America's most select and prestigious art schools. Pat's life was about to change. Until her graduation from Washington Irving High School, she struggled as a school girl, first a victim of failure and then a product of encouragement. Her art portfolio was expanding and her talent was beginning to be appreciated.

Regardless of Pat's emerging talent, her parents, the society of the time, and Pat herself saw only a typical American female whose future quite naturally focused on marriage, family, and home—most certainly *not* in a full-time career as an independent, professional artist. This next "conflict" in her life was just beginning, an internal struggle that would last for at least twenty years.

In that regard, the summer of 1951 was pivotal for the young artist. With her new art scholarship in hand, Pat's life seemed firmly dedicated to art. Yet she was plagued with deep-seated doubts about her academic as well as her artistic abilities.

Following her graduation from Washington Irving High School, she went to her mother's home in Mill Rift to make a "big decision."

Should she take a chance and go to college or settle into the traditional and safe woman's role and choose marriage?

According to her mother, Pat received a marriage proposal from a man who was twelve years her senior. Pat sincerely cared for this man and he was capable of offering her a good and presumably sheltered life.

It's difficult to know what her parents thought and how they advised her—a daughter whose learning difficulties at times had seemed so insurmountable. But finally, Pat herself decided.

Marriage could wait and she chose college in the vague hope of a "career" in the fine arts.

This is only one of many potentially costly investments in herself that Pat made purposefully— hard choices that still undergird her success.

THE COOPER UNION, Photograph, ca. 1953
Photograph of Patricia Buckley in class at the Cooper Union.

Pat was an enthusiastic student by the time she reached the Cooper Union.
Although she didn't always agree with her professors and was sometimes penalized
for her independent spirit, her years at this excellent school of art were profitable ones.

In this learning environment, many of Pat's views concerning life, religion, and art
came to maturity.

The Cooper Union was and is a
well-rounded training program for artists
and designers. It prides itself in its pursuit
of excellence in both the fine arts and the
mechanical sciences. It was founded in the
nineteenth century by Peter Cooper who
believed that art, industry, and good
design are indisputably linked.

This philosophy set the perfect
tone for a young artist who was already
demonstrating that talent involved
something more than just creating mere
aesthetics and pretty pictures.

In this milieu of great art
traditions that combined an understanding
of style with practical production methods, the young
Patricia Buckley was introduced to the work of a select
group of early modernists.

Pat Moss' art is filled with sophisticated
references to twentieth-century Expressionism. Pat
began to realize she was not alone in many of her anti-
academic reactions.

Earlier artists of the late nineteenth and
twentieth centuries, especially the French
Impressionists and the German Expressionists, had

rebelled against the academic restrictions of the established art world of their time.

These artists broke with tradition and created whole new systems of aesthetic thought and creativity. They laid a groundwork that combined freedom and insight with the hard work of creating an original style frequently based on revolutionary ideas.

While Pat was no revolutionary in the artistic sense of the word, her own ideas were often in contrast to the ideas of her teachers and peers. Her pleasingly stylistic renditions created almost entirely for the sake of emotional exuberance ran counter to the conventional academic canons of the early 1950's.

Like the Impressionists and Expressionists, Pat was ahead of her time in her belief that art didn't have to follow a set of definite rules, but was open to modification to fit specific moods and perhaps better please specific audiences.

Many of the distinctive components of Moss' very identifiable style can be traced to her years at the Cooper Union where her figure drawing abilities were developed and honed. Also, the professors at the

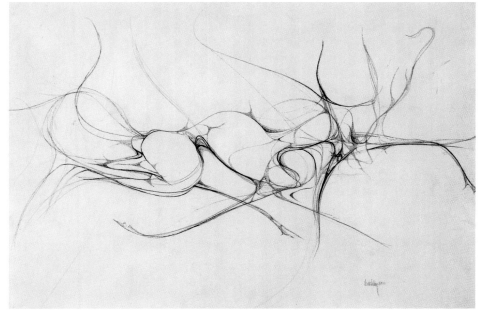

ANIMAL FANTASY, Ink, 15" x 20", 1953
An academic piece likely created as a classroom exercise at the Cooper Union.

A delicacy, an internal sensuality, a balance, and a love of what is called the cyma curve (an "S" line) are all present in this piece that is the precursor of all Pat's later art. To understand this piece is to understand much of what has been called the Moss Style.

Cooper Union insisted on balance and clear design in her work with no wasted decorations and unnecessary details. Good design was and continues to be a hallmark of this fine training school, and Patricia Buckley plainly took all such constructive advice sincerely to heart.

"The Cooper Union turned out to be everything that I had hoped for. From my very first day, I was aware of the atmosphere of professionalism that prevailed among our teachers and that affected the attitudes of all the students. We were students and yet we also were treated as artists. The staff respected the individual character of each of us; we were not made to conform but were guided in the evolution of our own styles. The teachers took a genuine interest in each of us and gave us enormous encouragement.

"Here my symbolism found acceptance. Here negative criticism was replaced with positive guidance. I now knew my art was valid, that it had a place in the world and that I would survive as an artist."

Nonetheless, Pat took even more to heart the heritage of her Catholic religion.

Remembering this period in her life, she later wrote that "From my religion I discovered the importance of tradition and how tradition and creeds can be best expressed through the use of symbols.

"This is how symbolism came to be an important influence in the evolution of my style. In my representational painting, I sought to express the true significance of each subject, be it a family, an animal, a landscape, a building, or whatever, by discovering its strongest spiritual characteristic and then painting that characteristic in a forceful symbolic form.

"When forced to paint in a realistic style, I found I had no heart for what I was doing and

COLOR FIELD, Mixed Media (watercolor, pastel, gold metallic paint, ink), 10" x 14", ca. 1955
A completely non-objective painting closely related to the Medieval-type illuminations Pat was using for her Aquinas "Book of Man" project.

With richly applied paints mostly within the deeper tones of the warm red spectrum, this color field painting is an academic piece full of emotional impact.

It is closely related to the work of a number of mystical-Modernist artists who were popular during the 1950s including Jackson Pollock, Morris Graves, Mark Tobey, Clyfford Still, Barnett Newmann, and even Mark Rothko.

If Pat had followed her Modernist inclinations without the influences of Medievalism, the world ultimately would have come to know a much different P. Buckley Moss.

inevitably I slipped back into my world of symbols. This had been my world through the most informative years of my early life.

"It was what I found worked and was the only honest form of expression for me. It was far more real to me than an imagery that portrayed only the outer skin of the subject."

Pat's realization of her own religious heritage and her deliberate expression of that heritage in her art came about primarily through her exposure to the translated writings and the intricate philosophy of the saintly founder of medieval Scholasticism, Thomas Aquinas. What this twelfth-century philosopher, theologian, scholar, and later canonized Saint of the Church had to say to a young twentieth-century would-be artist is at the core of what would later become the Moss phenomenon.

Pat was introduced to Thomas Aquinas by a contemporary theologian, Fulton Sheen.

She relates, "When I was at Washington Irving and during my days at the Cooper Union, Fulton Sheen, later the Archbishop of Rochester, New York, became my mentor. Late in the evenings after completing my homework, I would watch him on television. He had the gift of making it seem that he was talking to you and you only. Although I had never met him, I felt that he knew me and he became a special friend. Fulton Sheen has had a lasting influence on my

ON MAN WHO IS COMPOSED OF A SPIRITUAL AND A CORPOREAL SUBSTENCE; AND FIRST, CONCERNING WHAT BELONGS TO THE ESSENCE OF THE SOUL.

(in seven articles) question LXXV

Having treated of the spiritual and of the corporeal creature, we now proceed to treat of man, who is composed of a spiritual and of a corporeal substence. We shall treat first of the nature of man, and secondly of his origin. Now the theologian considers the nature of man in relation to the soul, but not in relation to the body, except in so far as the body has relation to the soul. Hence the first object of our consideration will be the soul. And since Dionysius says that three things are to be found in spiritual substance—essence, power and operation—we shall treat first of what belongs to the essence of the soul; secondly, of what belongs to its power; thirdly, of what belongs to its operation.

ST. THOMAS AQUINAS MANUSCRIPT ONE, Illumination and calligraphy from Thomas Aquinas' "Book of Man"—Overleaf, Ink, watercolor, gold metallic paint on parchment, 12½" x 24", ca. 1954/55
Patricia Buckley's senior project at the Cooper Union. Chapter featuring the Title Page from Thomas Aquinas' "Book of Man" (translated from a thirteenth-century source).

Pat's calligraphy and the illuminations are both based on a short section of the *Book of Man* by Thomas Aquinas (ca. 1225-1274). Considering Pat's religious convictions as well as her different style of learning, this project dealing with a religious philosopher who saw the world in terms of good and bad and soul and substance seems especially suited to Pat's artistic inclinations as well as her spiritual dispositions. Incidentally, both Aquinas and Pat opted for the good and the soul, which made them especially compatible.

In this specific title page with words like "corporeal substance" and "essence of the soul," the artist expresses the idea that immortal human souls emerge from the mortal human body as individuals and strive heavenward during their lives through saintly visages appearing out of the clouds of color. A later illumination in the book shows the clouds becoming a mysterious mass as God and the souls seem to join.

life and, although I am not a regular church goer, I do abide by many of the philosophies that I learned in the late hours of a long day. It was because of him that later at the Cooper Union I decided to transcribe and illustrate St. Thomas Aquinas' *Book of Man*. This undertaking gave depth to my religious and philosophical thinkings."

Thomas Aquinas (born ca. 1224/25, died 1274) originated a scholastic philosophical and theological system that became known as Thomism. Among many other things, he taught as Aristotle had stated that an artist received all of his inspiration "from the ideal image in his soul." According to Aquinas, such an ideal image came directly from God and thus was of indescribable value and incomprehensible goodness.

At the center of Aquinas' philosophy was his belief that human beings acquire a knowledge of reality through sense perception: *Omne quod cognoscitur per suam similitudinem vel per suum oppositum*— "Whatever we know, we know either by its analogue (something that is similar) or by its opposite."

Normally, people are able to "sense" the world about them by observing, touching, or whatever. This, according to Thomistic thinkers, leads first to the "law of similarities," a learning process in which one compares familiar objects, facts, and even common emotional responses to unfamiliar concepts in order to promote awareness, understanding, and a new level of acceptability.

To an artist, the process of creating relational similarities most often equals relevance—the making of images whose intended relationship to an audience is based on some degree of pre-existing information. Such images are intended to strike familiar chords with the rationale that if people know what they like, they will come to like what they know.

But what of immaterial things? So much of religion, which was Aquinas' concern, and so much of art, which was Pat's concern, deals with immaterial things like souls, feelings and emotions, and even God.

The Thomists concluded for various historical and spiritual reasons that the so-called "corporeal" (real) world was secondary to the more important mystical aspects of existence. For them, God was the principal cause of everything and the immaterial world was His domicile.

They reached this critical judgement both through what they called "negation"—proving what something is not (God is not a thing)—and through effect (when there is an occurrence, such as a miracle, that cannot be explained by reference to bodily causes). Consequently, human immaterial ("immortal" like God) souls make it possible for human beings to share in the immaterial acts of God such as thinking, believing, hoping, loving, etc.

In formal neo-classic calligraphy, Pat translated a short section of one of Aquinas' works entitled "On Man Who is Composed of a Spiritual and Corporeal Substance."

Her original illustrations accompanied the calligraphy. Thomistic "negation" and "effectuation" were both a part of this section which is ultimately a proof that the unseen soul—the spirit of the divine—gives reality and meaning to all human life.

This experience with the ideas of St. Thomas Aquinas became the basis for Moss' ongoing conviction

ST. FRANCIS, Etching/drypoint, 13¾" x 8½", 1953
An original print of Pat's interpretation of the great
Saint Francis of Assisi (thirteenth century).

Pat has always been devoted to St. Francis who
was known for his piety, his love for every living
thing, his kindness to sinners, and his dedication to
what he knew to be his mission in life.

Notice the small ugly bird the artist placed in
the good saint's right hand. Pat identifies this bird
as a reference to her own soul which at one time
she believed could be loved only by someone as
kind and as generous as St. Francis.

Of course this little bird can also be viewed as
a reference to the traditional belief that St. Francis'
preaching was so great, even the wild birds came
to listen.

in her art and in her life that
goodness is the antidote for evil.

Pat came to believe that
illustrating things of the soul—
internal reality rather than things
as they could be externally sensed
through physical reality—is, in
itself and for its own reward, a
powerful corrective to a
potentially unhappy life in an
imperfect world.

Although philosophy and
religion played a dominant role in
the development of Pat's art, at
least two other sources of inspiration grew from her
studies at the Cooper Union: Modernism and
Medievalism.

The first, Modernism, as has already been
noted, was an integral part of her everyday education.
Cezanne, Van Gogh, Matisse, and Picasso along with
other influential French Impressionists and German
Expressionists were the source of Pat's willingness to
use exaggerated forms and contrasting minimal colors.

These artists gave young painters of the modern
generation, including Pat Buckley, the intellectual
permission to disregard anatomical and structural
realities and to emphasize subjective emotions and
personal responses over any mere pictorial narration.
Much of the unique and often minimalist style of
P. Buckley Moss can be traced to these influences.

For example, Pat's work has often been directly
compared to one particular Expressionist: the Italian-
born painter, Amedeo Modigliani (1884–1920), a young
bohemian who worked in Paris most of his short and

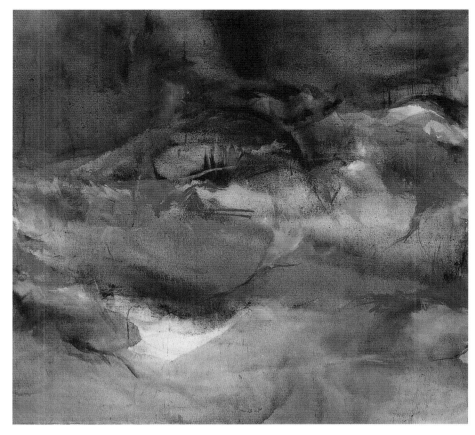

Here the artist combines the power of a religious icon with the elongated style reminiscent of the early twentieth century work of Amedeo Modigliani. In this combination, Pat joined the religious fervor of the Middle Ages with the free artistic expression of the modern age.

This subject, the Virgin Mary, obviously is very dear to Pat's heart since it represents a return to the artist's own religious upbringing.

Notice in the painting how the viewer's attention is drawn to the eyes of the Madonna—the traditional windows of heaven in any religious icon.

reckless life. In particular, he depicted the human form in a way that must have excited Pat's imagination. Modigliani's elongated faces with almond-shaped eyes, long tube-like necks, and drooping shoulders became common elements in the work of the artist who was to become known as P. Buckley Moss.

On the other hand, it was the influence of academic Medievalism that directed Pat's attention towards rational order and popular meaning in her art. Otherwise, she might have been merely another non-objective, self-centered, angry art school graduate. Encouraged, of course, by her Thomastic belief in the power of the soul, the Medievalism of Patricia Buckley primarily took the form of artistic storytelling.

RHYTHMIC LANDSCAPE,
Oil on Canvas, 46½" x 45", 1955
An Impressionist piece painted in Mill Rift, Pennsylvania, soon after Pat left the Cooper Union.

This piece represents the artist's emotional impression of a late fall landscape—the soul of nature.

While the piece is academic, it doesn't lose touch with popular reality.

From Pat's school years to the present, much of her art tells an unending story. She uses her invented characters—originally Catholic saints and later the Amish—to appear and reappear in her paintings and prints. They tell a story about life, values, and relationships, and more particularly about love, happiness, generosity, loyalty, and caring.

This kind of narrative presentation relates pictorally to the art of a number of late medieval and early Renaissance scene painters, most notably Hieronymus Bosch (1450-1516) and Pieter Bruegel The Elder (ca. 1525-1569).

Bosch illustrated subconscious phobia while Bruegel The Elder depicted archetypal actions. Both artists used a narrative plot-like format. Bosch, however, was famous for his depictions of strange highly stylized, humanoid figures whose actions controlled the mood of his works. Here seems to be a direct correlation between Pat's elongated and often bow-legged men, her ethereal women, and even her moppet-

FLAG GIRL MOPPET/ FLAG BOY MOPPET FIGURES, Watercolor, 3" x 2¾" (girl), 3" x 3¼" (boy), date not available Two delightful representations of moppets—Pat's images of "humanoid" children.

Representing happiness, charm, innocence and a host of other virtues, these honest and simple symbols elicit a smile.

like children and the curious but always meaningful figures employed by this late-Medieval master. On a more visual and compositional level, Pat's art seems more like the work of Bruegel The Elder. These similarities may be coincidental; however, based on the fact that both artists subscribed to Aquinas' soul-centered philosophy, many common threads appear including the importance of forms, control of colors, and the arrangement of horizon lines to suit the needs of their mutually mystical outlooks.

In addition, both artists add generic architectural details intended to draw the souls of their viewers into the soul of their respective artistic creation.

Another Medieval feature that has almost instinctively become a part of Pat's art is her use of what is called the "lancet arch" design. This arch, closely related to Gothic architecture, became for Pat, as it was for many Medieval cathedral builders,

a reaching up to God. It has remained one of her favorite forms and the basis for the composition of many of her most popular works of art.

In addition to everything Medieval mentioned above, Pat's portfolio has been filled for many years with a variety of Madonnas and mother-and-child paintings. Such paintings were common before and during the Middle Ages. Like Pat's contemporary versions, these works were historically intended to be both devotional and representational.

For example, in a modern Moss Madonna, viewers may refer specifically to the Virgin Mary and her Christ Child. However, if such an idea is too "holy" or too "Catholic," they can approach the same work as an idealized comment on either motherhood or womanhood. The artist usually remains non-committal, though her own religious background and interests are always apparent.

HOW CALM THE MORN, Watercolor, 14½" x 28", 1978
A quiet piece filled with internal meanings.

The quantity "three" has both mystical and religious connotations. In this work, the three egg shaped forms (the egg represents new life) contain some of Pat's best-known Valley Style symbolic devices including the generic house, the flat Amish carriage and horse, and the crystal-clear reflections.

A Moss generic house never has doors and is a reference to the idea of the Medieval spirit or soul house.

The artist uses the passing Amish silhouette-like carriage to connote the passage of time.

The crystal-clear reflections (always minus any human references) are based on Thomas Aquinas' observation and belief system that souls (as seen in the reflections) are more significant than the supposed reality from which they emanate.

ETERNITY, Etching,
13¹/8" x 10¹/2", 1988
An original print of a
Mennonite couple standing
under a lancet arch.

The arch supports a flowering
climbing vine. As the title
implies, the couple stand
together representing an
eternal promise of support
and loyalty.

Finally, it is fascinating that one of Pat's most popular and endearing symbols can be traced to the Cooper Union and the artist's interest in Medievalism.

Drollery-black-cats, who always look out at the viewer and seemingly ignore the action of the painting or print, are a favorite bit of contemporary Moss painting. That these delightful creatures have their roots in the early Middle Ages is a surprise to many Moss collectors.

This symbol—or icon—comes from a time when illiterate or modest and often monkish artists "signed" their works by drawing curious little animals meant to look out of the artist's work into the world of the living. Such cats, or drolleries as they're more correctly called, were substitutes for the artist through which he/she could watch forever those who might be looking into the make-believe world of the artist's work.

Although the Cooper Union years were obviously a time of intellectual growth, philosophical consolidation, and artistic development for the young Patricia Buckley, these years were also often very difficult for her personally.

Pat again lived at home on Staten Island and commuted daily into Manhattan. Her home life continued to disintegrate as her father was invariably inebriated by the end of the day and her parents fought constantly. Pat's younger brother Danny was still at home. However, her older sister Mary, whom the family

CATS GALORE,
Silkscreen, 9½" x 18¼", 1993
A humorous study of many
Moss drolleries.

Thirty-seven whimsical cats
look at the viewers who are
looking at all the cats.

called "Honey," had escaped the situation through marriage. It was a depressing predicament for the young would-be artist and her schoolwork suffered. Teachers noticed; Pat Buckley lacked concentration and suffered from an inability to produce the kind of creative work expected. Finally at the end of her second year, Pat was told that she could not move on without repeating the year's academic program.

This struck a serious blow to Pat's ego as well as to her chances of professional advancement. It also meant that she would not be able to participate with her classmates in the annual summer art field trip. Pat's

bitter sophomore year ended with a summer job waiting tables at the Big Win Inn on the Lake of Bays in Miscoka, Canada.

Pat later wrote about that summer away: "Far from home and in the company of people who knew nothing of my problems, I got my life back into perspective. At the end of eight weeks I went back home with renewed energy and in much better spirits."

BLUE CRUCIFIXION, Oil on Canvas, 42" x 48", 1955
A strong artistic and religious statement summing up the artist's training and experience at the
Cooper Union.

The traditional reference to the three crosses on the Hill of Calvary and the centered Christ-
cross as seen in this piece were to become the models for many of Pat's later works. A tree up
front, a "witness tree," was to become one of the artist's most characteristic symbols. It was Pat's
way of referring to the ancient "Tree-of-the-Cross" redemption concept (a solid symbol of hope
in an ever-changing world).

    This piece is still in the artist's private collection. She considers it to be her talisman.

CHAPTER THREE
Emerging Artistic Developments

A Rustic Virtuoso Patricia Buckley received her "Certificate" for completion of prescribed courses from the Cooper Union in June of 1955. Considering her interests, her training, and her philosophical position, one can understand why her earliest professional works were academic in style and usually outwardly religious in subject matter. As a well-trained artist, her professional potential seemed to rest in the rather limited area of religious art.

Despite later comparisons to Grandma Moses and various other untrained folk artists, this young artist was not and never could be the kind of untrained naive artist who paints freely only what is remembered or what is imagined. She was not and is not a folk artist in any sense of this much misunderstood title.

From the beginning, Pat resolved to become a significant contemporary religious artist who would be painting well within the great traditions of Western art. This was her ambition.

Then she met Jack Moss when he was working as a waiter at a hotel near her mother's home in Mill Rift, Pennsylvania. Jack was a young chemical engineering student from Florida.

Their courtship moved slowly at first. Pat later wrote that Jack "was very easy to be with. Being with

THE MOSS FAMILY, photograph, ca. 1973 A photograph of Pat and her family about 1973.

Pat's family from left to right: (back) John, Jack Moss, Pat Moss, Mary, (front) Becky, Ginny, Chris, and Patty.

him was so much better than having to be at home with all the problems." Their friendship grew into love and two years later on April 8, 1956, a year after finishing at the Cooper Union, Pat and Jack married.

The dutiful new bride immediately turned her attention to her husband's career, to homemaking, and to child bearing. And children came—six in a row: on October 29, 1957, Mary Elizabeth "Liz"; on January 5, 1959, John Damian; on June 15, 1961, Rebecca Louise "Becky"; on December 7, 1962, Patricia Ann "Patty"; on February 12, 1964, Virginia "Ginny"; and finally, on April 23, 1966, Christopher Vincent "Chris."

A series of moves occurred in close succession. The family first relocated from New York to New Jersey; then to Delaware; then to a mobile home park

BOATS, Oil on board, 8" x 9¼", dated 1967 A palette-knife piece likely influenced by Gulf-side scenery near Port Arthur, Texas.

This piece was probably painted about three years earlier than it is dated, since Pat often reworked earlier pieces and re-dated them for specific exhibitions.

While this is an academic piece, it shows Pat's interest in creating an overall and visually understandable pattern without actually referencing either earth or sky.

This refined mood piece is said to have caught the attention of the art show judges who awarded it a blue ribbon.

near Boston, Massachusetts; then in February, 1961, to Port Arthur, Texas; and finally, in 1964, to Waynesboro in the Shenandoah Valley of Virginia.

Although her growing family took up much of her time, in 1976 Pat was named "American Mother Artist of the Year." Socially, Pat tried to help her husband along, especially after he went to work for Texaco in Port Arthur.

Pat and Jack bought their first house, put in a yard, and planted gardens. Pat became president of her Driftwood Garden Club. Between entertaining Jack's business associates, entering into the life of her community, and taking care of her growing family on her husband's limited salary, little time remained for the creative life of an artist. However, the talent and desire to create art persisted. In her life as Mrs. Jack

Moss, it was the hope of earning money rather than lofty philosophical ideas that finally motivated Pat to resume painting seriously.

By the time she had arrived in Waynesboro, Virginia, with a husband in a new job, five children, and a newly rented house to furnish, the money situation was critical. Although Jack had a good job at the local DuPont Lycra plant, there was never enough. In response, Pat began to make the amateur-artist rounds.

As Pat recalls, "We now had five children and the problem was to find a house that provided us with sufficient space. After a lot of looking, we rented an unfurnished farmhouse outside the city limits. We moved in with very little in the way of furniture and when Jack would go to work, I set out to look for beds, bureaus, mirrors, tables, chairs, and all the kitchen needs. Someone told me the best bargains were to be found at country auctions, and I drove up and down the valley looking for them—bargains were a necessity with five children and another on the way.

"I had never been to an auction before, and at my first one I must have looked pretty naive. I assumed that what was being offered was in good condition, and when I wanted something I made it very obvious by calling out.

"At lunchtime, I got into conversation with a Mennonite who, in a gentle round-about way, told me how important it was to do a thorough examination of each piece of furniture before the start of an auction. He instructed me there was often more to be learned about a piece of furniture by looking at its underside than by looking at the top, and he suggested that I should try to make my bidding less obvious. Before the auction restarted, he went with me to check over three pieces I was very interested in.

"That afternoon I sat with a group of Mennonites, and so started an association that has lasted to this day and that has had a profound effect on my life and philosophy."

The usually quite unsophisticated patrons of weekend sidewalk art shows and seasonal crafts festivals provided the amateur artist with a source of ready cash.

They came, they saw, they liked, and they bought—it was a situation that began to position P. Buckley Moss as a popular producer of salable art.

Moss' new neighbors, the people of the Shenandoah Valley of Virginia, could not be expected to be receptive to all the ideas of an academically trained and profoundly thoughtful artist with real talent.

SHOWALTER FARM,
Watercolor, 11¾" x 22½", 1973
An example of P. Buckley Moss' early Valley Style painting.

Tranquility, limited color spectrum, a variety of horizon lines, minimal details, trees up front, thin-wash painting—these are all characteristics of the Moss Valley Style.

Showalter Farm was located in the Shenandoah Valley about three miles west of Waynesboro, Virginia.

Sadly, the house was torn down and the barn greatly renovated about 1980 after a business development took over the farm.

In time, local people grew to accept and even love the hard-working wife and young mother whose art they believed they understood, really understood. Hazel Dunlap, a member of the local garden club, took Pat under her wing and began to accompany her to various sidewalk art shows. Robert Kerby, another early Waynesboro friend, helped her promote her art locally. Civic leaders such as Dr. Thomas Gorsuch (later the mayor of Waynesboro), his wife Fran, and J.B. Yount (a local attorney) began to collect Pat's work and commission special paintings from her.

These people and many others appreciated Pat's efforts to produce affordable art that promised to make their lives more beautiful. They rewarded the young artist with

their friendship and their continuing patronage.

Pat Moss' solution to dealing with people whose expectations were not especially her own had been played out once before when as a very intelligent and sensitive child, she either consciously or subconsciously dismissed academics in favor of dreams. At that time, the expectations of her mother and the nuns as well as the pain of her unhappy family life caused her to retreat into her own imagination.

Now, as an adult and a well-trained artist from New York City, she faced a potentially hostile, strongly southern, and aesthetically innocent public. Pat repeated the process that had been her creative salvation as a youngster: she delved into her own fertile imagination. This time, however, Pat was unable to take her new neighbors and future collectors along with her into a fresh world of artistic fantasy.

The paradox of the Moss Valley Style was born—Patricia Buckley Moss literally re-made herself as P. Buckley Moss, creating a style of painting that was acceptable to her new public at the same time it remained true to her background and interests.

This metamorphosis brought people into a relationship with her work by presenting them with friendly and positive pictorial analogues—pictorial similarities to a life which many of her admirers feared they had somehow lost.

Moss made the past live again for many people, if not in reality in the modern Valley of Virginia, at least through an acute sense of pure nostalgia which she was able to present over and over to an almost voracious waiting public.

Pat's memories of this time are especially insightful: "Throughout the time of having my babies, I continued to paint. I was of course far too busy to think of doing anything serious about marketing my work, and much of what I painted in those years I gave away to family members and friends.

"Having a large family, which with Chris's arrival, totaled eight, money was short. When the children wanted presents to take to other children's birthdays, I would paint a painting.

"I remember how upset they used to be saying, 'Mommy, this isn't a proper present. I don't want to give this. It will look silly.' At Christmas time, I made all our Christmas cards.

"As word got around about my paintings, people started to come to the house asking if they could buy from me. At the suggestion of a friend, I entered some paintings in an art show being organized by the Waynesboro Chapter of the Virginia Museum. One of my pieces won first prize, and as part of the prize I was given a one-person show.

"At that show, every piece I exhibited sold. With this encouragement, I started to show my paintings in exhibitions further afield. Often I would take the children with me. Sometimes this would be popular with them, particularly if there was some other excitement in the town where we were exhibiting, such as a circus. I would then leave them at the circus and go and stand by my paintings."

On October 30, 1966, Pat wrote in her diary: "5th Sunday Tea was today—*Liz* won a first and *Crucifixion II* won a second—meaningless awards from meaningless people—my work looked beautiful—I loved each piece." At first, Pat's blunt opinion of exhibition judges and art-show awards seems abnormally harsh for a woman whose art usually is filled with positive affirmations. But Pat's sense of approval extends to all of her art, not only to an arbitrarily designated list of winners.

Her diary entry bespoke confidence in her own talent and ability to create visually satisfying expressions that transcended any single critical opinion, informed or otherwise. For Pat Moss was meant to succeed in the arts, and all opinions that might otherwise inflate or diminish her own confidence had to be, especially for her, truly meaningless. She loved and still loves her art, all her art.

Aside from just a few personal comments, Pat primarily used her little notebooks as a means of keeping track of the names of her art works as they were either sold or traded.

For 1966, Pat's carefully handwritten lists indicate a general continuation of many subject areas she had pursued since her Cooper Union years.

St. Francis, Monk, Crucifixion, Madonna, Miniature St. Peter, and *Angel* all illustrate her longstanding religious interests while names such as *Sunset, Miniature Landscape, Horse and Trees,*

VALLEY FARMERS,
Watercolor, Dimensions not
available, 1977
A fully-developed Moss
Valley Style piece.

The painting is filled with her
meaningful symbols
including a tree up-front, an
Amish couple, oval
reflection ponds, a basket of
apples, a pail of sticks, and
her quintessential multiple
horizon lines.

    As is typical with all of
these pieces, it is impossible
for a viewer to know exactly
where the artist intended the
earth and the sky to meet.

    The Moss Valley Style
has become one of the
most popular original styles
to have ever been created
by an American artist.

SKATING PARTY—Overleaf, Watercolor, 28" x 60", 1982
A tour-de-force in Moss' Valley Style.

One of Pat's most popular scenes, this large painting is a rich assemblage of some of her best iconographic images including the witness tree up-front, the Amish, two generic (doorless) houses, a wind blowing from many directions as indicated by the skaters' scarves, the clear reflection of objects versus the total lack of reflections for people, the clean winter snow, and a pair of observant geese with their feet hidden by the snow.

To summarize these references in order, a tree refers to eternity as in the case of the tree-of-the-cross or a family tree; the Amish symbolize honest people living a life of integrity; the generic houses are Medieval spirit houses (abodes of the soul); the multi-directional wind is a biblical reference to the Holy Spirit blowing as it may; the reflections of the building and the lack of human reflections come from Aquinas and refer to the difference between mortal souls (buildings, tree, rocks, and animals) and immortal souls (human souls which are only seen by God); the pure snow and the pair of geese (minus their feet which once were believed to be an allusion to sin and evil) symbolize everything from Providence to loyalty.

Blue Barn, *Winter Landscape*, *Reclining Horse*, *Mad Hatter*, *Guitar Player*, *Sails*, and *Potted Flowers* represent Pat Moss' wide variety of traditional artistic subject interests.

Then, in March, 1967, a new subject-interest appeared in her list of available paintings. For the first time, Pat recorded a piece containing the word Amish in its title: *Amish Men*. It was priced at $100, but she traded it to a Mr. Reiback for "9 BOOKS."

The following June, Pat sold a piece entitled *Amish Children* for $24. It was the seventy-sixth piece she had sold within the year and the first Amish-titled piece for which she received cash. From that point on, Amish pieces became more and more frequent. In October, six of the twelve pieces that she either sold or gave as gifts had Amish in their title.

Thus the Valley Style was born: a combination of traditional academic subject matter with unique Valley of Virginia symbolism. Populist in spirit, friendly and familiar in intention, it combined the rural scenery of the Waynesboro area with images of the distinctive Plain People whose communities were at the time located near the Moss' Waynesboro home. Although the Valley Style of P. Buckley Moss is closely linked to all the influences that came to the artist during her childhood, her training years at the Cooper Union, and her adult experiences to date, the compositional balance and freshness of the style makes it very adaptable to the print medium. Perhaps this indicates a new influence at work within the artist's sphere of reference.

It has been suggested that the Valley Style is somehow related to Oriental art, especially to Japanese woodblock prints of the nineteenth century. Pat remembers being impressed by the Japanese collections displayed at the Freer Gallery of Art in Washington, D.C. Something about the Oriental sense of limited colors, the brush-stroke flow of light and heavy lines, the conventionalized linear patterns, and the storytelling thrust of traditional Japanese prints moved and influenced Pat.

While her Valley Style is certainly not Japanese, its elements speak with a voice that is as well understood and appreciated in Japan as elsewhere, in much that same way the great Japanese print artists of old spoke to the people of their day and age.

Within a few short years of the style's inception, people from many other rural areas inhabited by the

Amish began to claim Moss' Valley Style as indigenous to their own regions. Collectors from Pennsylvania, Ohio, Indiana, and Iowa all saw their picturesque rural countryside in the body of Pat's work. However, the farms, hills, ponds, broad valleys with wintertime trees, and ever-present Plain "Amish" People of this Style evolved from scenes the artist first knew and loved in rural western Virginia.

The people in black and other simple attire who occur time and again in Moss' Valley Style were originally inspired by two Plain communities located near the artist's Waynesboro home.

A small Amish settlement was located in and around Stuart's Draft, Virginia, just south of Waynesboro. In addition, there was and still is a larger community of Old Order Mennonites about twenty miles away from Dayton, Virginia. Though slightly different in attire and lifestyle, both communities descended from German and Swiss Anabaptist immigrants. Their strict religious beliefs were formed in the Radical Reformation of the mid-sixteenth century. In keeping with other Anabaptist settlements situated throughout the country from Pennsylvania to Arizona, the Virginia groups kept to their old ways by the clothes they wore, by refusing to use modern conveniences such as automobiles and electricity, and by living together in independent, well-organized, and closely-knit communities.

When Pat Moss first came in contact with her new neighbors, they seemed to her to be a Christian anathema: anti-Catholic heretics whose religious heritage was far different from her own.

It was only later as Pat became acquainted with what to her were strange ways and novel beliefs that her admiration for them developed and grew. This admiration seems to have been related in part to the feelings she had once reserved for the Catholic saints whose lives she had studied at St. Clare's. These saints of old were presented as models of the godly life, examples to be imitated as one made one's own way through the perplexities of life.

According to Pat, "As my contact with the Mennonites increased and I learned more about their way of life, the greater my admiration for them became. I had grown up a Catholic and I had been true to that faith and had done my best to practice its disciplines. Many of my paintings were of religious subjects, crucifixions, paintings of the saints, and Madonna-and-Child subjects. These were symbols of my religion and a medium for expressing my faith.

FOR THE BIRDS, Oil on board, 24½" x 17⁷⁄₁₆", 1976 This oil painting is presented in a modernist style reminiscent of some of the work of Pablo Picasso.

With a Mennonite boy enthroned on a stool and surrounded by fancy caged birds, this piece makes an artistic statement about freedom and containment.

The boy (like the birds) is contained in his cage by a religious tradition exemplified by his plain clothing.

Nonetheless, this piece also elicits a feeling of freedom in the bright face of the boy as well as in the open beaks of singing birds. The message is that reasonable containment and freedom of expression are not mutually exclusive.

"Now I was meeting people of a different faith for whom my traditional symbols were not a part of their religious tradition. The Amish gather in a neighbor's home to worship, while Mennonite churches are modest in construction and bare of ornamentation.

"And yet everywhere I found expressions of the simple faith of these plain people. It was in their work ethic, in the diligent husbandry of the land, and in their dedicated care of their animals. It was in their mutual support and in their caring for one another. It was also in their love and caring and respect for the elderly. From their common name, the 'Plain People,' I originally had imagined them as being rather quaint and somewhat dull. This name could be misleading, and yet in reality it is very appropriate. If you take the word 'plain' to mean devoid of what is superfluous and ostentatious, it perfectly describes the core of a lifestyle. The honesty and sincerity in all aspects of their life make it very comfortable to be among the Plain People.

"The people you meet are the people you meet and they do not coat themselves in a protective outer

MY HANDS TO THEE,
Watercolor, 27⅜" x 9⅝",
1979
This piece is a statement of faith in the integrity of hand labor.

A Mennonite quilter inside a lancet arch design is surrounded by a house and children waiting against the fence.

veneer while pretending to be somebody other than their true selves.

"This example made a profound impression on me. I saw that these people living their uncluttered and uncomplicated lives were enjoying a full measure of life's gifts and life's fun. Strong in family, strong in loyalty, successful through their own hard work, these Amish and Mennonite people remind us of the price that many of us are paying for today's primarily materialistic attitudes.

"The beauty of the Valley and the message that I saw in the lives of the plain people directed me toward making them the subjects of many of my paintings. By painting the scenes of their everyday life, I am making my own statement in support of a more simple and honest lifestyle."

For P. Buckley Moss, the new images of Amish and old order Mennonites slowly became images of "living saints" whose lives of faith apart from the sins of the modern world were the equivalent of holy Medieval icons through which the faithful could look beyond the grave and toward the glories of heaven.

These highly stylized representations immediately caught the attention of the artist's public. Many people found the plain-clothed, stick-like images to be quaint and cute. They adored the artist's optimism and they felt an affinity, sometimes real but often imagined, to the places that were pictured and especially to situations that were suggested.

From its beginning, Moss' Valley Style was a popular success.

GOLDEN JOY, Watercolor, Dimensions not available, 1984
A tour-de-force, this popularly styled piece incorporates some of the artist's best-known and best-loved symbols.

The work's power lies in its ability to convey a whole array of traditional concepts with simple visual references. The meaning in this painting of the couple, the children, and even the witness pair of geese is obvious—all are references to the family and its lasting integrity as a human institution.

In addition, Moss has included apples and sticks—items with a slightly more veiled meaning. For example, the apples in the man's basket specifically represent hard work and perhaps the threat of evil (based on the meaning of this symbol as the forbidden fruit in the Garden of Eden). These apples of life can be contrasted with the apples of youth, ripe fruit, in the basket of the little girl. While the former suggests experience, the latter is a traditional artistic reference to innocence.

The bare sticks in the little boy's hands create another interesting allusion. Here however the implication is more historical than biblical. In the early sixteenth century, Raphael painted similar sticks in his "Marriage of the Virgin" as emblems of Joseph's bachelorhood as well as of his impending marriage to the young Virgin Mary.

In Raphael's painting, Joseph's sticks are beginning to bloom in contrast to sticks held by Mary's other suitors. In Moss' painting, her little boy holds his bachelorhood in the same way that his sister holds her maidenhood—with promise for the future.

This painting is one of Pat Moss' most idealistic and optimistic celebrations of the basic family unit. Although it is art and not genealogy, its message of joy and hope seems to be universally understood, even by those who cannot themselves share in all the elements of its utopian memory.

CHAPTER FOUR
Life As An Artist

Enjoying the Dance Since the early 1970's, the creative life of P. Buckley Moss and much of her personal life, has been ruled by her devoted following of admirers. Pat is called the "The People's Artist" and this title, for better or worse, now determines her artistic direction.

Her art has become primarily the people's art, and like the great masters of the Renaissance who diligently painted for their lordly patrons, Pat Moss paints diligently and ever faithfully for her patrons—people that know, appreciate, and ultimately (though indirectly) commission.

Modern reproduction printing is the primary culprit as well as the paramount impetus for Moss' curious situation. In the beginning, the public could invest in original works of art at reasonable prices. As the popularity of P. Buckley Moss soared, so did the prices for the very limited supply of original art. In order to meet the demand for her art, Pat began offering signed, numbered, limited edition, offset prints.

At first they were a novelty product issued by the artist herself, but they later became the very serious products of her

JOHN AND MARY, Watercolor, 42½" x 44", 1979
The popular style of P. Buckley Moss.

Even the name of this piece adds to its popular appeal. Similar in composition to Grant Wood's famous "American Gothic" painting, this piece depicts a conservative farm couple with a baby posing in front of a typical Shenandoah Valley two-story stone-block farmhouse.

Marriage is the intended theme of this piece and references thereto can be found throughout its composition. Even the drain pipes in the background, becoming one as they cascade down the side of the house, can be taken as a matrimonial reference.

Naturally, the couple proudly displaying their little offspring in a basket used for collecting eggs (customary symbols of new life) are the primary proof of the marriage theme. Notice the sticks in the young man's hand—they're beginning to bloom. Like the baby, these sticks are a traditional reference by the artist to new life and perhaps even to fertility. It is probable that at the time Moss painted this piece she was thinking of one of the most marital-centered pieces in all history, Raphael's masterpiece, "The Marriage of the Virgin" (1505). In this monumental work, Raphael used sticks, blooming and otherwise, to express the greatness of the event he was depicting: the union of The Holy Family.

company, P. Buckley Moss, Incorporated (subsequently changed to P. Buckley Moss Galleries, Ltd.).

Despite the practical intrusions of her business and the well-meaning demands of her collectors, Pat Moss continued to pursue her ideal of the perfect art. Positive optimism, friendly associations, easily recognizable symbols, harmonious colors and lines, and the courage to uphold traditional moral and ethical values became the popular hallmarks of her art.

On a merely visual level, much of the art of P. Buckley Moss took on a rather predictable look. In time, people began to expect a Moss to look like a Moss in subject as well as in style. People felt comfortable with what they understood and didn't want to be challenged by art purchased purely for enjoyment.

Thus, already an excellent artist, Pat Moss also became an excellent communicator. She recognized an unexpressed need in her collectors and she was in a position to meet that need. In time, her ability to communicate deeper meanings through her art, even to people who were otherwise disenfranchised from the main stream of contemporary art, is the nucleus of her success, especially in the very lucrative area of reproduction prints. Pat Moss speaks subconsciously to people of all walks of life in a way everyone seems to understand. Pat Moss' distinctive vocabulary of symbols has become immediately recognizable and instinctively appreciated by literally millions of devoted admirers. For many, the messages delivered through the symbols of Moss' art have become more real than reality itself. They actually seem to transfer their own emotional concepts of reality into the fabric of her work—similar to the scholastic process that Aquinas called "similitudinem" (recognizable similarities).

Pat's remarkable ability to consistently achieve this amazing feat meets her seemingly paradoxical goal of producing a simple art with deep mystical connotations. The power of her work is such that she has the ability to make people feel that she has created her art "just for them."

Even so, such a warm and friendly dialogue between a congenial artist and her dedicated collectors is not the end of the creative process, at least not for Pat Moss. At her most profound level, significant and awe-inspiring meanings occur far beyond mere symbolism, past anything which is obvious and easily articulated.

Consider, for example, the symbol that comes closest to being Pat Moss' logo emblem: a pair of Canadian geese. At some point during the artist's

LORDS OF THE REALM,
Watercolor, 31¼" x 31¼", 1981
A Moss logo piece: two Canada
geese in a winter scene.

In ancient mythology, wild geese
served as mediators between
heaven and earth. In that role,
they represented the will of the
gods, divine providence,
expressed for the benefit of
human beings. Pat Moss'
Canada geese are among her
strongest symbols. They represent
God's beneficent judgement in a
world that needs goodness and
understanding. Also, because
geese supposedly mate for life, a
pair of wild geese always refers to
loyalty, especially marital.

Moss geese almost never
have feet. In art, birds' feet
traditionally symbolize sin/evil
primarily because they're scaled
and clawed which somehow
gave them demonic
connotations. Pat's geese are
purified symbols of her own idea
of Divine Providence.

development and training, this ancient symbol was
brought to her attention. True, for most people a wild
goose is just a large bird that lives in or near the water
in a gaggle and flies south for the winter. But, for Moss
and for historical and cultural iconographers the
painted symbol of a goose means more.

For Pat, geese came to symbolize many of the
virtues she has long held sacred. When Pat learned that
the ancient Egyptians, Greeks, and Romans considered
the goose to be a mediator between heaven and earth
(the gods and human beings), and that the early
Christians, especially her own ancestral Celtic
forbearers, looked on wild geese as God's own
messengers, i.e., figurative illustrations of missionaries
and evangelists, she gave them a presence with an

almost divine-like
status in her own art.
They witness
goodness, integrity,
and faith in her art.
In addition, wild
geese symbolize
loyalty—especially
marital loyalty. This
optimistic message
wasn't lost on Pat
and is one she passes
along to her viewers.
Throughout her work, she subtly shares historically-
based symbolic meaning.

Re-consider the wild geese and the fact that Pat
never shows their feet. For her, the feet of wild geese
are a symbol whose meaning evolved from the Middle
Ages when they were associated with the dirt of the
earth versus the freedom of the sky, the scaling of
diseased skin versus healthy flesh, and the claws of evil
versus caressing hands. In summary, the feet of geese
became symbols of a devil whose sinful power held in
check what was otherwise pure nobility. Pat's geese
don't show that side of their ancient symbolism.

Considering the artist's religious and philosophical inclinations, the tendency in her art towards a deepening of spiritual considerations is quite understandable.

Naturally, she's interested in attracting new collectors and in increasing the success of her company, but Moss' most authentic incentive to paint is her conviction that it's through art, and especially her art, that the heartfelt doctrine of positive thought and helpful affirmation can be spread afar.

Within the pictorial content of Pat's familiar symbolism exists a rich world of two-dimensional references that are inexplicably united to the cultural, mythical, educational, and religious traditions of the artist. These subliminal messages are carried by the unpretentious art of P. Buckley Moss, messages their creator believes have the potential to change and improve the world.

The profundity of such an iconography is difficult to measure. Subjective analysis is almost impossible. Likewise, some art critics have ignored Moss' iconographic inclusions while verbally damning the artist for what they see as catering to popular tastes. What Moss has done is to invent a world of images filled with philosophical observations and questions.

The question of "How many angels can dance on the head of a pin?" may seem out of place in the late twentieth century. Regardless, to Moss and to many like her who hold to the mysteries of their strong religious convictions, such a question still has immeasurable spiritual ramifications. Moss' art states the ancient propositions of beauty, justice, and truth, the accumulated wisdom of the ages in ways her audience can understand and perhaps begin to consider. So let the angels dance in Moss' art and in the heads of those who are able to look into that art and see beyond the absurdities of the obvious.

However, it is not only because P. Buckley Moss directly or indirectly affects the conscious and subconscious sensibilities of her patrons that she has been called a phenomenon. Some give her this accolade because of her talent, her originality, her prodigious output, or even her enormous popularity.

But behind all the tributes, probably most people call her a phenomenon because of her financial success. Moss is financially successful which is attributable to painting art that is in demand.

Moss' art has been formally exhibited at several museums in the United States and in Japan at Tokyo's Metropolitan Museum.

THE FISHERMAN, Oil on canvas, 47" x 35", 1990 Completed for Pat Moss' exhibition at the Metropolitan Museum of Art in Tokyo, Japan, and the cover piece for the exhibit catalog.

Though this oil painting is dated "1990," the artist states that she spent about twenty-years working and re-working the details of the piece. She recalls that it probably began as a portrait of St. Francis which she later changed to St. Peter. At that time, she added the subject's bright orange hair and the reddish background (the fiery clash of colors is historically and biblically symbolic of the Apostle Peter's explosive personality).

Its current title refers to St. Peter as a real fisherman who was called to become "a fisher of men."

Limited edition prints of her paintings hang in private homes, offices, and other places of business from the Atlantic coast to California. Today Moss is represented by more than 300 dealers nationwide. She is assisted by an ongoing publicity effort supported by the Moss Portfolio and the P. Buckley Moss Museum.

In 1986, Pat Moss was awarded her first honorary Doctor of Fine Arts degree from Centenary College in New Jersey. She received a second honorary doctorate, Doctor of Humane Letters, in December, 1993, from the University of Akron.

Then, on May 12, 1996, Pat was honored again in her own Virginia backyard when Bridgewater College, located only a few miles from her Waynesboro home, awarded their distinguished neighbor a second Honorary Doctorate of Humane Letters. Patricia Buckley Moss, the little girl whose teachers thought she couldn't succeed even in grade school, was three times a Doctor!

In addition, in 1986, a few dedicated Moss collectors formed the P. Buckley Moss Society. From its beginning, the Society has attracted members because of the popularity of Pat's art. Society membership pins containing enamel examples of popular Moss images have become collector items while members-only special print offerings are an important membership incentive.

Nonetheless, the Society's current goals aim far beyond the world of art as evidenced in the organization's motto, *for the love of children*, reflecting its still evolving charitable thrust into the field of special education for children with learning difficulties such as dyslexia.

In 1989, Pat Moss published her autobiography—a delightful combination of insightful anecdotes and philosophical observations which has been especially helpful and inspiring for parents of children with learning disabilities. Illustrated by the artist, its primary message is that if Pat Moss can do it, with hard work and measurable goals anyone can achieve a measure of success.

Pat Moss herself remains the force behind almost everything done in the name of P. Buckley Moss.

Pat and her first husband Jack had grown more and more apart as her artistic success grew. She wrote in her autobiography, "I am a strong-willed person driven by an obsession to paint. This force took over the life of my husband and me, and progressively altered the equilibrium of our relationship. I believe that Jack would have been happier had we lived a conventional life with him as the principal breadwinner and decision maker. For my part, I was at a stage in my life and my career in which I needed not so much the physical support of labor as the intellectual support of discussion, criticism, and shared vision. The break up of our relationship was a traumatic experience for both of us. To go

through it takes a great deal of courage. It is much easier to stay where you are than to go through this crisis in your life. If Jack and I had stayed together, we would have deprived each other of much of the fulfillment of the later years of our lives. Both of us are

THE ARTIST, photograph, 1981
Pat Moss in a dreamy mood in her new Georgetown gallery (Washington, D.C.).

The artist is shown with paintings of two of her favorite subjects, a sensual horse and Canada geese.

THE HENDERSONS,
photograph, ca. 1984/85
Mr. and Mrs. Malcolm
Henderson striking a formal
pose in evening attire.

For a number of years, Pat
and Malcolm have regularly
hosted formal charity
fundraising events.

now remarried to partners whose energies and interests match our respective aspirations. Both of us are living full and productive lives again."

In 1979, Pat and Jack were divorced and in 1982, Pat married her business manager, Malcolm Henderson. In many ways Malcolm is the perfect complement to Patricia Buckley Moss. He's an active extrovert while she remains a compensating introvert. He's a dare-devil entrepreneur while she's a creative conservative. He's the life of the party, a showman in his own lifestyle, while she's actually quite shy, often quiet, and very sensitive. He's a wizard with words, a writer who can imitate others' verbal styles, including his wife's, in his own writing.

Pat, on the other hand, while quite an articulate and entertaining public speaker, is still primarily visually focused. Malcolm prepares most of her letters and gives Pat outline notes for her speeches, but as he says, "Although she carries them to the podium, she never uses them and takes her own course, omitting much of what I hope she will say and including many excellent points I had not thought of."

Despite his behind-the-scenes role, Malcolm Henderson is responsible for much of Pat's public persona—the P. Buckley Moss people flock to see and

experience at every opportunity. Pat and Malcolm form a team and from the first meeting, they naturally belonged together.

The late 1970s and early 80s were times of personal trial for the artist. Her separation, divorce, and remarriage led to strained relationships with her six children and the Roman Catholic Church, as well as the on-going disapproval of her devout Catholic mother. Pat's ability to think positively was put to the test again when she was struck suddenly with breast cancer and subsequently had a mastectomy. "For a few hours after the operation I thought I was going to die, even that this was the Lord's punishment for having failed in my first marriage. Then I thought of all the paintings I had yet to paint and all the plans Malcolm and I had yet to fulfill, and I sent for my paints and began to work again from my hospital bed.

"Five days later I was flying to Denver to keep an appointment to open an exhibition of my paintings; there was no time to wonder about the future."

CHILDREN'S MUSEUM CAROUSEL, Mixed media on paper,
24½" x 27¼", 1985
A celebration of childhood.

Children from various ethnic backgrounds ride the lively carousel animals. Filled with
activity in its colors, its tactile surfaces, its sweeping horizontal lines broken by fixed
verticals and most importantly, in the near rapture of its subject matter, this piece
stands as a visual demonstration of the artist's youthful enthusiasm for life.

Pat survived, went back to her painting, made peace with her children and her mother, remained a catholic with a small *c*, and subsequently joined the Methodist Church.

These same years were a time of growth for Moss' business interests. Pat acknowledges, "Under Malcolm's management, the business grew at a fast pace. I had always enjoyed meeting my collectors and now the opportunity arose to travel for appearances at gallery shows. When Charles Kuralt made me a subject for one of his programs in 1988, he described me as 'The People's Artist.' He talked about the very large number of people who come to meet me at shows. For me, being described as the people's artist is the greatest of compliments. Painting is a form of communication, and that a large number of people respond to my communication means that I am doing my job well and fulfilling a need.

"An artist has to spend a lot of time alone working in the studio. In my case, for the most part I am painting subjects that narrate human behavior and relationships. When I go to my shows, I am able to witness people's reaction to my work.

"Their reactions act as stimulant, and give me the encouragement and energy to go on. A show is like the opening night for the concert soloist; after months of rehearsal, the moment comes to present yourself to the audience and hopefully hear the appreciative applause."

Under the continuing leadership of her business manager Malcolm, P. Buckley Moss, Inc. became P. Buckley Moss Galleries, Ltd. and The Moss Portfolio, a marketing and distribution organization. While Pat continued to paint in her usual and prolific manner, Malcolm began the work of consolidating the company's financial security and establishing copyright protection for the artist's images. William Speakman, a bright accountant, was brought into the organization and his management company was contracted to assist Malcolm in

VICTORIAN ROW,
Etching from an edition of 99, Plate size 17½" x 20½", 1987
An excellent example of Moss' etching ability.

This two-plate piece was printed from a background tonal plate for colored inks and a foreground black plate for black ink. Moss created the plates at her etching studio in Montreal, Canada. Etchings are considered to be the finest original multiple prints available and are unique works of art. No two pieces even from the same edition are ever exactly alike.

Etchings are printed on wet paper in greasy inks from reverse-image metal plates prepared by the artist using acid and acid-resistant compounds, cutting and spreading tools, plus an assortment of complicated mechanical procedures to achieve the desired result. Etching editions are small in number and precious.

the everyday affairs of the company. Bill's business acumen brought a new orderliness to Pat's company.

About the same time, Joshua Kaufman of Washington, D.C., was retained as Pat's copyright attorney. Management was firmly in control, thanks to Malcolm, Bill, and Joshua. Pat Moss, artiste extraordinaire, would not be exploited by anyone whose intentions or actions might damage either her reputation or her ability to create art, or the value of her art to her collectors.

Using the unique and easily recognizable images of Pat's art, Malcolm began to expand the company's product line.

Since the offset reproduction prints were already a great success with editions regularly selling out, Malcolm felt it was time to provide their collectors with more Moss in more avenues suited to meet their needs. In that regard, early in 1981, P. Buckley Moss Galleries, Ltd. signed a major publishing contract with Anna Perenna, an American company with German/Bavarian roots, to produce a series of Collector Art Plates. Klaus Vogt, the President of Anna Perenna, already had established an excellent reputation for his company among serious plate collectors. For both Anna Perenna and Moss, the new

agreement turned out to be a fortuitous event. Pat's images and colors translated well from watercolor to porcelain to reach fresh audiences of eager collectors. Series after series of the highest quality art plates were produced with a goodly number of individual plates from various series receiving International Plate Awards at major plate collectors' conventions.

P. Buckley Moss prints, art plates, and, later, figurines were followed by dolls and other licensed products such as cross-stitch designs from June Grigg and a collection of gift items including a journal, address book, and inspirational and other books published by Landauer Corporation of Iowa.

The exposure from all these products has brought greater name recognition as well as greater demands on Pat's time and attention.

Considering her immense popularity, the diversity of her artistic responsibilities, and her very busy schedule, it is amazing that Pat is still an actively-creating artist.

As has been said, she is a prolific artist. Although not all of her works are intended to be masterpieces, modern masterpieces continue to come along regularly in her paintings and especially in her work-of-art etchings.

Pat's art soars whenever her thoughts return to the soul-centered references of her twelfth-century mentor, Saint Thomas Aquinas.

Etching, the so-called king of the printer's art, has emerged in her life's work as the perfect medium for some of Moss' most sublime artistic expressions.

During the past decade, Pat has made innumerable trips to Montreal, Canada, where she works in the etching studio of Paul Machnik. It is usually there, although sometimes at Pat's own etching studio in Florida, that Paul and his wife Mewa and Sye, a talented Laotian, assist Pat Moss in the difficult and demanding task of creating detailed single and double plate etchings.

Etching is not easily mastered; it requires a thorough knowledge of a complicated process including the scarring of a matrix (a metal plate) with acids, rosins, and burins, and the blending of different colored inks.

Pat Moss is a fine etcher who ably brings an abstract idea through the whole creative and mechanical operation to become a hard-won and finely-polished original print.

When Pat can afford the demands of this very time-consuming process, her finished etchings communicate with the spirit of Aquinas' mysticism as well as her own aesthetic verve. Probably more than any other art form, original etchings make Pat Moss' clearest statement about what it means to her to be a twentieth century artist, an eternal optimist, and a devout believer.

CHAPTER FIVE
Solitude for the Soul

A Place Apart Pat Moss is an artist who usually doesn't require a specific setting in which to do her work. She has always been able to draw and paint wherever she is, whether in a hotel or on an airplane, or simply at home. As long as she has her tools and some peace and quiet, she can create.

Nonetheless, a dream of someday having a studio of her own, a place apart in which to "spread her mess" and make art, has long been Pat's dream.

Some of Pat's earliest memories are of doing her drawings at the kitchen table as part of a quiet family gathering.

While other family members read the newspaper or books or did homework, Pat drew pictures of horses and other things that interested her. She was the one member of the family who didn't seem able to read and just didn't like to do what she considered to be usual schoolish pursuits.

From childhood on, Pat took advantage of every available opportunity to establish rudimentary studios in which she could work. One of her earliest studios away from a school setting may have been at her mother's home in Mill Rift. Pat herself insists that this specific studio never existed and attributes it to a figment of her mother's imagination.

The truth of the studio story is probably unimportant. What matters is Pat's relationship with her mother and her mother's memory of taking an active role in Pat's creative development. There is no question that Pat's mother, Elizabeth, was and continues to be an inspiration for her daughter. Aside from any usual mother/daughter relationship, Pat's visits to Elizabeth's design studio/office in downtown Manhattan became significant memories and possibly goals for the young would-be artist. Although Pat acknowledges that her mother at times was not an encouraging agent during her years of struggle as a troubled student, Elizabeth today is as proud of her artist-daughter as any mother possibly could be. In retrospect, Elizabeth wishes that she had recognized Pat's talent earlier and that she could have been Pat's champion, helping her more directly to overcome some of those early challenges.

During her twenty-two years of marriage to Jack Moss, Pat's studio tended to exist merely in corners of otherwise activity-packed rooms within her usually crowded household.

Only after they moved to their second Waynesboro home near the city's Country Club could Pat create a dedicated work space for herself.

The fairly new two-story ranch contained a large basement. As Pat became known as an artist in her area, her portfolio of paintings increased accordingly.

For her Waynesboro home, Pat designed a family room at the front of the house and created a separate basement room which became her first formal studio. Still, her numerous paintings seemed to be scattered throughout the house in both finished and unfinished states.

People who knew the Moss family in those days speak fondly of informal parties in this house where the wine was in the kitchen and the guests moved through the house, upstairs and down. Paintings were always available to purchase. Pat rarely gave a piece of her art away; and she still tells young artists to "always value their art and to give it the respect of having someone pay for the honor of owning it." Although she is very generous with people in need, her generosity with her paintings invariably comes from her own desire of the moment rather than from any external prompting.

The Moss household was not exactly a Bohemian existence. Although Pat says she kept her house "neat as a pin," she describes her own studio as "chaotic."

Regardless, the noise and activities generated by six children, a "DuPont" husband, and an artist mother could hardly have been viewed as a model of planned orderliness.

Although the suggestion of potential chaos didn't seem to bother Pat, in 1976, she began making plans for creating a place of her own, a "hidy place" as she called it, where she could work out her artistic ideas and projects in relative peace and quiet.

At one point or another during these years, she noticed an old apple-packing barn located not far from the new and larger third Waynesboro house to which the family had moved. This barn was situated at the edge of what had been an orchard on a slight rise above the nearby South River. The owners, an old Waynesboro family, hoped to develop the area as a fine subdivision which in time would be called Loving Acres.

Pat, who was finally beginning to experience some monetary success, made an offer for the old barn and five acres of surrounding property. Her offer was accepted and the new life of the P. Buckley Moss Barn/Studio began.

According to local tradition, the Barn was built as an animal and hay barn about 1915 and converted into an apple-packing barn about ten or fifteen years later. It remains a typical Shenandoah Valley braced-beam bank barn, strategically built into a hillside so its

EVENING RUN,
Watercolor, 8¹⁄₈" x 32¹⁄₈",
1978
A typical Moss Valley Style
piece filled with the
ambience and the tension of
a cold winter's day in the
countryside.

The background structure in
this piece is a typical
Shenandoah Valley bank
barn built into the side of a
hill, quite similar to the old
barn that Pat remodeled to
become her extraordinary
home and studio.

Although the feeling of
peace dominates the mood
of the painting, it also offers
a contrasting sense of
excitement and even
movement. The feeling of
tension held in check is
attributable to at least three
factors: first the introduction
of a sensually-portrayed
horse image painted in red
spectrum colors against an
opposing blue spectrum
background; then the
definite breaking of the
generally horizontal restful
composition of the piece
with an over-sized vertical
image (the horse, in this
case, doesn't even fit inside
the general composition of
the piece); and last, by not

providing her viewers with a
clearly defined single horizon
line, consequently
allowing their attention to
intentionally wander across
the plane of the entire
painting.

These significant
attributes are typical of all
Pat's best Valley Style
paintings. They make her
work singularly distinctive
and set Moss far apart from
the merely pictorial and rural
depictions produced by
many of her closest
imitators.

lower floor can be entered at ground level from the river side while its upper second floor has a ground-level entrance on the opposite side. At the time of its purchase, the barn had endured over sixty years of hard use.

Despite discouraging remarks by local citizens and the refusal of some contractors to consider her barn project, Pat Moss finally persuaded a local builder, Tom Lucas to go ahead and begin transforming her disintegrating apple-packing barn into a usable studio. Pat herself designed the all-important metal-pipe super-structure that would ultimately support the

barn and keep it standing. And since she didn't want to destroy the old building's wonderful feeling of openness, the interior supports remain entirely visible.

The renovation of the barn was completed about the same time that Pat's marriage to Jack came to an end. For the saddened and soon-to-be single artist, it was a short walk from her previous home to her new Barn/Studio.

Everything Pat had so carefully and aesthetically planned for the Barn now became the setting for her new life. It was her place apart...and a new beginning.

WEDDING DAY, Watercolor.,
39¼" x 59½", 1982
Malcolm and Pat on their
wedding day.

The painting that Pat Moss
created to celebrate her marriage
to Malcolm Henderson has all
the characteristics of the Moss
Valley Style.

HAYSTACK ROCK,
Watercolor, 9¾" x 30¼", 1988
An impressionistic depiction of
Haystack Rock, a natural stone
formation located on the Pacific
Ocean off Cannon Beach,
Oregon.

Splendid and somewhat
academic, the painting is one of
Pat's favorite pieces. It
exemplifies the artist working in a
style other than her Valley Style.

Four years later, Pat and Malcolm were married in the Washington Street United Methodist Church in Alexandria, Virginia.

Later, they celebrated their wedding with a gala reception for friends and relatives at her Waynesboro Barn. Pat had created a large painting for over the brick mantel entitled Wedding Day.

The bricks in the painting continue from the brick floor in the barn entrance. The color of the brick in the barn, repeated in the fireplace, and finally carried into the painting represent Pat's own life—its connections to her Barn/Studio, and its hopes for the future in the representative Amish-style couple standing proudly in the center of the work. The Barn and this painting are a centrifugal force within the P. Buckley Moss phenomenon.

Although Malcolm loved the Waynesboro Barn and probably would have liked living in Waynesboro, he was still co-owner of The Atlantic Gallery in Washington, D.C., and because that was his place of employment, the Hendersons also maintained a city house in the Washington, D.C., suburb of Palisades.

While never considered to be their primary residence, it served as a base for the developing Moss Galleries, Ltd. and gave Pat and Malcolm a place to stay near the company's new headquarters, first in

downtown Georgetown and later just across the Potomac in Falls Church, Virginia.

The Palisades house is an off-white contemporary structure that occupies most of its relatively small off-street lot. On the back side of the house, numerous windows afford a view of an intimate fenced garden. Pat's easel was usually set up in front of the windows where she maintained one of her most private studios.

On the wall she hung only one Moss original: her watercolor study of Haystack Rock, a quiet academic piece that depicts a mountain-like boulder standing alone at the edge of the Pacific Ocean just off Cannon Beach, Oregon.

GOLDEN DUNES,
Watercolor, 10" x 18", 1996
An example of Pat Moss
painting in her Florida-style.

The exotic animals and
birds of the Gulf Coast, the
flat horizons, and the
extraordinary pinks of
Florida's sunrises and
sunsets seem to appeal to
Pat's aesthetic tastes.
   Paintings done in this
style form a distinct grouping
apart from her more popular
Valley Style pieces.

Although the huge rock dominates the scene, the artist has included the minuscule image of a couple walking along the sandy beach. The privacy of the couple and the privacy of the Palisades house both reflect the same mood of modest tranquility and sophisticated dignity.

Pat's image was best served by her Barn, which remained hers and Malcolm's ostensible home until 1986. During the ensuing years, a small picturesque cottage was built adjacent to the Barn on its eastern side. This was for Pat's mother to use while visiting. It was soon called Gran's Cottage, though it was also used by the Moss children who had a large dormitory on the cottage's upper floor.

The entire Moss complex—the Barn, the Cottage, the well-manicured lawn leading down to the river, and the property's open fields and woods—eventually amounted to twenty-two acres. It soon became and remains a popular place to visit, especially for Moss devotees and others interested in contemporary, adaptive restoration architecture.

Despite the possibility of escape to Georgetown, the demands of what were becoming overly enthusiastic fans drove the Hendersons more and more often away from Pat's Barn.

Pat had to paint, and the free-for-all ambiance of her great architectural creation as well as her own spiralling celebrity status

became, at least in part, an impediment to her work. She would, of course, keep the Barn—it had become an important part of her personal life and public image— but from 1986 on, it would be used only for special events as well as for some singular family occasions.

In 1986, Pat and Malcolm officially moved to St. Petersburg, Florida, where they had purchased an impressive pink stucco house built in a mid-1920s version of a tasteful Venetian villa. The house is located at 501 Brightwaters on fashionable Snell Island. They also purchased a commercial gallery in a handsome Modernist/Latin/Art Deco-style building near downtown St. Petersburg. For a time, it appeared as if Pat and Malcolm would move all their interests to Florida.

For a time, there was even talk of starting a Moss Museum in St. Petersburg.

The Snell Island house offered Pat another chance to change the interior of an aging structure into a comfortable and contemporary home. Her improvements remained true to the original design, and subsequently she received an award from the local preservation society for her efforts. Pat's distinctive touches can be seen throughout the house, from the creation of a Florida room facing Tampa Bay to an open style of decorating that makes the house feel both friendly and cool. The Snell Island house was a natural party house with plenty of room outside for tents and service tables on its broad bayside lawn.

Why and when the Hendersons' interest in Florida began to fade is unclear. Both Pat and Malcolm developed some good and lasting friendships with neighbors. Pat loved the light, and from her small studio on the second floor, a series of pink-glow watercolors emerged. The exotic animals, trees, and plants of Florida were joined to her on-going Valley Style. For a time, it looked as if Florida would become a "new Virginia" for P. Buckley Moss and her Company.

The Hendersons' move to Mathews County, Virginia, happened over a three-year period culminating in January, 1995, with the relocation of the Moss Portfolio Distribution Center to Mathews from Falls Church, Virginia. The principal attraction of Mathews is the natural friendliness of its people and its proximity to salt water.

PAINTING LESSON,
photograph, 1997
Pat shares her studio with
several young artists, Sarah,
Katherine (Kate), and
Shawn Donnelly.

For Pat, it is a delight to
introduce children to the
world of art, especially when
they are her grandchildren!

Located on a low-lying peninsula on the western side of the Chesapeake Bay between the York and the Rappahannock Rivers, the town of Mathews sits in an old established area of Virginia that has been settled since the seventeenth century. Its small crossroads villages are peopled mostly with fishermen and farmers and a smattering of outsiders who are either vacationers or retirees.

Pat and Malcolm located in Mathews primarily because of Jake Henderson, Malcolm's son who heads the distribution and publishing part of P. Buckley Moss Galleries, Ltd. Jake and his wife Betsy, who had family roots in eastern Virginia, first acquired a vacation home about 1989 in Mathews.

Some time later, Malcolm visited this retreat and was immediately attracted to Mathews with its flat vistas across open water. In 1993, Malcolm bought an old fishing cottage which he extensively remodeled as his own getaway. Shortly thereafter, Pat bought her own house across the road from Malcolm's and began her own remodeling project. Soon, what had been a straightforward late nineteenth-century two-story farmhouse was transformed into a very livable studio/home. The house stands alone on a large lot, overlooking a brackish creek not far from the Chesapeake Bay. In 1995, Pat purchased another house just across the creek, which she remodeled as a place for her mother when and if she decides to leave Mill Rift, Pennsylvania.

Since she has become a successful artist and a celebrated personality, the life of Patricia Buckley Moss Henderson continues to dance between her widely-recognized public personna and her private—often intensely private—longings.

Even when she's at the center of her image, for example at her Barn in Waynesboro during one of her regular Open House extravaganzas, she's privately wishing to be alone in one of her hidden-away studios in Washington, in Florida, in Mathews, or in Waynesboro. (The public studio at the Barn is augmented by a quieter studio in its basement which is used when the upper floors are occupied by her mother or "the children.") It's where she wants to be. "Every hour I'm awake and not cooking or fiddling with something, I'm here (in my studio)."

While Pat's life may be in conflict between who she is and who people think she is, her art escapes any sense of tension. With almost boundless energy she often extends her workdays far into the night. Her productivity is astounding.

THE BLUE HORSE, Oil on
canvas, 45" x 45", 1989
An abstract side view of a horse,
the painting is displayed at the P.
Buckley Moss Museum and an
especially favorite piece of those
who have either studio or art
history training.

Its colors and lines as well as its
rich textural qualities make this
piece a strong statement for the
entire iconographic meaning of the
horse. As a symbol of youth,
strength, sensuality, and
masculinity, this writhing equine
speaks volumes about both the
dark and light sides of the
human psyche.

Amazingly, Pat's painting and limited-edition
prints represent the sum total of her contrasting
experiences. She pours all parts of herself into them.

People continually ask Pat just how long it takes
to complete one painting.

"Sixty-four years," P. Buckley Moss answers
promptly. "It requires all my years and all my
experience to finish every piece."

THE PLATES

CRUCIFIXION, Aquatint, 9¾" x 7", 1953

An original print from Patricia Buckley's college days at the Cooper Union.

This aquatint is an especially powerful expression of the young artist's religious fervor. It also expresses what was to become a long-standing artistic interest in using arrangements of undulating lines to convey a wide assortment of emotional moods.

The piece, in contrast to many of her later pieces that use flowing horizontal lines to create moods of peaceful relaxation, is highly charged into a primarily vertical arrangement. In *Crucifixion,* Moss [then Buckley] uses cyma-reversa/cyma-recta curves ("S" lines) to alert her audience to the work's sense of tragedy and pathos. Only the arms of Christ and the "branches" of His cross interrupt the work's generally upward flow, breaking the rhythm and creating the sorrowful tension associated with the Crucifixion.

From the historical/biographical collection of the P. Buckley Moss Museum.

**TREES AND BARN, Oil on canvas, 16" x 49",
ca. 1966/67**
A forerunner of the P. Buckley Moss Valley Style.

Trees and Barn combines some of Pat's earliest impressions of
the rural scenery of the Valley of Virginia with her academic
sense of the flow of color and lines. Except for its
recognizable details—the trees and the barn—this piece is
close to the artist's earliest pure color-field paintings (see
Color Field, No. 11).

From the collection of the DuPont Employees Credit Union,
Waynesboro, Virginia.

AMISH GIRL, Gouache, 6" x 3½", ca. 1967/70
An unsigned and undated portrait which is elegant in its simplicity.

This and the following piece are among the earliest examples of P. Buckley Moss' paintings of Amish subjects. They are painted in a relatively academic style whereby the artist has used a thickened watercolor to create definite lines and visually rich textures. It's as if the artist suddenly noticed the purity of the lifestyle of the young subject as she was caught by the artist in a furtive backwards glance.

From the collection of the P. Buckley Moss Museum.

AMISH BOY, Gouache, 13¼" x 3½",
ca. 1967/70
An unsigned undated full-length portrait of a
somewhat shy young man.

Although similar to the previous piece, this
depiction contains a boldness suggesting *Amish Boy*
was painted a year or two later than *Amish Girl*.

The textured watercolor effect of this piece—
gouache—is quite noticeable and important to its
overall artistic content. The artist uses a shadow
outline around the head and shoulders of the boy
to push the clear blacks of his hat and coat away
from the mottled background.

Interestingly, on the back of the artist's board
on which the piece is painted, Moss wrote
her address along with the original price of this
piece—$25!

From the collection of the P. Buckley Moss Museum.

EXOTIC CHILD, Original print/chromolithograph, 9¾" x 6½", ca. 1965
A richly embellished piece filled with exotic details.

Exotic Child is closely related to many of the academic pieces painted by Pat while she was a student at the Cooper Union. In fact, if the piece were not signed "Buckley Moss," it would have been automatically consigned to her school days.

There is something very nineteenth-century about this painting. The artist's attention to detail and the exotic mood the piece radiates relate it to some of the late Romantic artists of the pre-modernist generation.

Although Pat Moss was never a pure Romantic artist, much of her interest in nature and storytelling and her refusal to be a slave to photographic reality place her in an academic category not unlike many of her late nineteenth-century artistically Romantic forebearers.

From the collection of the P. Buckley Moss Museum.

THE MUSICIAN, Pen and ink, 11⁷⁄₁₆" x 8", 1969
P. Buckley Moss working in a "Cubist" style.

The Musician is an excellent example of the influence of a leading modernist artist, Pablo Picasso, on the work of P. Buckley Moss. The subject, a nude playing a guitar, is one that Picasso himself explored. In Moss' version, the shy maiden wearing only a hat of ribbons peers nervously off to her right as she slips from her precariously positioned Windsor chair toward what seems to be an equally precariously positioned vertical rag rug.

A sly humor is written all over this piece. Although Pat obviously admires much of what is good about "Modern Art," she refuses to take Cubism very seriously. She can do it with pleasant results, but it's a tongue-in-cheek experience for the artist as well as the viewer.

From the collection of the P. Buckley Moss Museum.

Waynesboro Choral Society

WAYNESBORO CHORAL SOCIETY PROGRAM,
Offset print, 7½" x 5", 1971
A lively print created for the cover of a Waynesboro Choral Society program.

When Pat Moss first came to live in Waynesboro, she almost immediately became involved in a number of civic activities including community choruses and community theatre. Pat created many poster and program images.

This one is especially noteworthy because of the enthusiastic and appropriate presentation of its subject. One can almost hear the voices blending, just as the artist has blended the singers' images into a symphony of neat dots and intricately curving lines.

From the collection of the P. Buckley Moss Museum.

MADONNA AND CHILD, Watercolor, 16½" x 12½", 1971
Before the advent of her Valley Style, Pat's most recurrent subject of the Madonna image.

Whether it was because she was the mother of six young children or a devout Roman Catholic, Pat's Madonnas (or are they self-portraits?) dominate the pages of her earliest journals.

The simplicity of both color and line make this an especially lovely piece. Here no tension exists between vertical and horizontal lines such as in her crucifixion drawings and paintings. Instead, rounded curves sweep in and around one another as the circular structure of the painting works itself outward from the middle to its rounded exterior lines.

Pat Moss is totally comfortable with this form of drawing and painting, and it shows.

From the collection of Mr. and Mrs. Yale M. Brandt, Chester, Virginia.

ORCHARD SCENE, Watercolor, 21" x 31", 1973
A straightforward and popular P. Buckley Moss subject matter.

By 1973, the year in which *Orchard Scene* was painted, Pat had established herself as a friendly sidewalk artist whose paintings could please even those folks who were not artistically inclined. Her references to the scenery and the plain lifestyle of the Shenandoah Valley pleased people who felt that contemporary art excluded them. The art of Pat Moss was understandable, nostalgic, and even inspirational. With pieces such as *Orchard Scene,* she was becoming known and the ranks of her collectors were growing.

From the collection of Mr. and Mrs. Ronald W. Wix, New Castle, Delaware.

TWO DOVES, Watercolor, 58" x 37", 1973
Two doves are the primary subjects of a peaceful landscape painting.

Although doves or pigeons are not usually considered to be elegant birds, Pat Moss' seem to be different. Artistically, these feathered friends lead the viewer into the work-of-art, passing along the row of trees to the large barn set on the distant hill.

These ordinary pigeons by Moss set a mood of serenity and hope that almost equate these birds with spiritually endowed doves of Medieval art. This artist masterfully takes the commonplace, gives it meaning and importance, and makes it appear to be a unique event.

From the collection of E. J. Lapsley, Waynesboro, Virginia.

SAILING, Watercolor, 10½" x 9", 1978

An intriguing and realistic watercolor painted by Moss in the great tradition of Winslow Homer (American 1836–1910).

During the late nineteenth-century, artists such as Homer made watercolor a respectable artistic medium. They found it especially well-suited for capturing the moods of nature, particularly where rapidly changing seascapes were involved.

The natural transparency of watercolor and its inherently spontaneous nature have made it the usual medium-of-choice for P. Buckley Moss.

From the collection of the P. Buckley Moss Museum.

EGG HORSE BOYS, Mixed Media (watercolor/pastel), 13¼" x 5", 1974
An Easter painting expressing the artist's own understanding of the grace-filled life.

By 1974, the year this work was completed, Pat Moss had adopted images of the Plain People—the Amish and the Mennonites—as one of her primary artistic subjects. Although she never depicted them individually by identifying them as actual characters, she used their distinctively costumed presence in her art to express values and virtues which she deemed to be corollary to their religious lifestyle.

In this piece, which is actually one in a series of *Egg Horse* pieces (from 1968 to about 1975), Moss seats two appropriately dressed Amish boys on a balloon-like horse. This horse image—or icon, as is more germane to the subject-at-hand—suggests the human life force (mainly human passions).

In art, literature, mythology, and even in modern psychology, horses have been used to symbolize youth, strength, sensuality, and masculinity. Notice, however, that two decorated Easter eggs support Moss' horse.

Eggs, and particularly Easter eggs, symbolize new life and resurrection. Consequently, by combining the eggs, the horse, and the Amish boys, Moss implies that the Amish (represented by the two boys) ride out life's passions (represented by the horse) because of their faith in a risen Lord (represented by the Easter eggs) and their steadfastness to what has become a very traditional set of beliefs.

From the collection of the P. Buckley Moss Museum.

KATHLEEN BEATRICE, Watercolor, 5½" x 3½", Early 1970s

A formal portrait of the painting's owner, Kathleen H. Beatrice.

Using only simple lines and a restricted number of colors, Moss produced a remarkably character-filled likeness of the subject. This was likely an early commissioned piece.

From the collection of Kathleen H. Beatrice, Lynchburg, Virginia.

BOYS ON DONKEYS, Mixed media, 23¾" x 59½", 1976

A full-blown early example of a major painting in the Valley Style of P. Buckley Moss.

In this piece, the two boys are dressed in the style of the Old Order Mennonite people of the Valley of Virginia. The barn in the background appears to be the typical bank-barn found throughout the Valley. Painted primarily in watercolor, the single tree up front and the series of horizon lines typify Moss' distinctive and popular style.

From the collection of Betsy Drake Hamilton, Greenville, North Carolina.

SIX WOMEN VISITING, Watercolor, 9" x 19¾", 1976
A painting with all the essence of popular Moss themes.

The essential Moss popular painting: friendly, well-designed, nostalgic, basically humorous, and allusively meaningful, painted with an economy of both line and color.

From the collection of Jane and Jack Marquis, Atlanta, Georgia.

MENNONITE GIRL AND BOY, Watercolor, 14⅛" x 11", 1978

A sensitive creation.

In this painting, Pat uses the elements of simple composition to create the feeling of a comfortable and relaxed relationship between the two human figures, a young Mennonite girl and boy. She emphasizes this feeling by placing the vertical figures against three horizontal fence rails and then draws her viewers into the young couple's conversation with the flat brim of the boy's hat. It's almost as if the viewer overhears the private communication of the young couple!

From the collection of Mary Lou Evans, Bluefield, West Virginia.

**QUILTERS AND CHILDREN, Watercolor,
Dimensions not available, 1978**

*A large watercolor combining scenes of two quilters at work and
of a boy playing the fiddle for an audience of five girls holding
baskets of apples.*

The aforementioned scenes are shown in a niche framed by
what appears to be stenciling, giving the piece a traditional
American folk-art appearance.

What does it mean? Knowledge of the basic philosophy
of P. Buckley Moss helps one to understand. Pat's tendency to
extol the honest work ethic together with her utilitarian
philosophy of art likely motivate the themes in this work of
art. Utilitarianism and the importance of the work ethic are
on-going ideas in the popular work of P. Buckley Moss.

Quilters and Children celebrates work, creativity, and
utility. In the scene at the top, two busy quilters create an
object of beauty and utility. Below, five little girls with
baskets of apples listen intently to a boy playing his fiddle.
Together, the apple pickers and musician symbolize the idea
of hard work.

Their products—a quilt, entertainment, and palatable
enjoyment—are presented within the tradition of the
nineteenth-century founder of the art school Pat attended,
Peter Cooper of the Cooper Union. They express Pat Moss'
inherent belief that the arts should not be entirely separated
from the real world where function and form are usually both
at their best if they are closely related.

From the corporate collection of the Coca-Cola Company of Atlanta, Georgia.

WARM WINTER MORN, Watercolor, 8⅛" x 16", 1978
A simple linear piece depicting a bare tree silhouetted against a dramatic winter landscape.

What remarkable contrasts in this piece! As its name implies, *Warm Winter Morn* is a mood piece that captures the feeling of a sudden change in what must have been a frozen landscape. Using warm reds set along retreating horizon lines, the artist has established a sense of abrupt warmth which vividly contrasts with the balance of the scene. One can almost see the snow melting and feel that warming breeze.

From the collection of the P. Buckley Moss Museum.

**SKATING FAMILY, Watercolor, Dimensions
not available, 1979**
An encyclopedia of wintertime activities.

Two up-front witness trees frame the entire scene depicted in
this obviously large painting. Adults and children, all in plain
dress, are skating. In the background, two boys ride
horseback while other children enjoy sledding. A Valley of
Virginia bank-barn crowns a distant hill.

    This piece, so full of activity, is expressed in the popular
style of P. Buckley Moss—the Valley Style at its finest.

From the corporate collection of the Coca-Cola Company of Atlanta, Georgia.

MOTHER LIGHTING CANDLES, Watercolor, 14¼" x 11¼", 1979
A solemn and meditative painting.

A Mennonite woman lights candles as two young children observe. The woman's hands are raised as if blessing the new light…almost in the Jewish tradition. A lancet arch encloses the scene.

From the collection of Joanne Friedman, Norwich, Connecticut.

APPLE ANNIE, Watercolor, 24" x 16", 1982

A full portrait of a prototypical young female by P. Buckley Moss and an example of the ever-popular Moss human image.

This image has been repeated time and time again in both its female and male form by Moss. Consider the C-shape of the subject's legs; the high waistline; the blue dress balanced with its white apron and pinafore; the basket of apples; the hooked arms; the stick neck; and the curly orange hair—certainly not realism per se.

Moss is a genius at constructing meaningful images and communicating their meaning to a wide audience.

Annie is one such image. This young girl means action (with legs like springs); hard work (with gathering arms for apples); and steadfastness (with a neat dress, a noticeably stiff neck, and a particular beauty enhanced by her distinctive hair).

The artist introduces the viewer to a friendly person easy to identify with and, consequently, to love.

Apple Annie is a passage into art, not merely a way of life.

From the collection of Teresa Bigelow-Telles.

OWL, Watercolor, 12" x 10", 1983
A fairly realistic drawing of a lone owl perched on a branch.

Although Pat uses owls as symbols of wisdom in their usual iconographic application, for this particular painting she's more interested in the owl as a wild creature of the night.

Pat and her husband Malcolm are dedicated supporters of the Wildlife Center of Virginia. The wild animals they've seen being nursed back to health at this facility have greatly influenced Pat's art. This painting is one such example.

From the collection of the P. Buckley Moss Museum.

SUMMER WEDDING, Watercolor, 24⅛" x 19¹⁵⁄₁₆", 1983

A ceremonial P. Buckley Moss painting intended to commemorate an important event such as marriage.

The essence of summertime conveyed in this watercolor is outstanding. In part, the artist achieves this feeling through the use of color, especially in the flowers included in this piece. Used either as a record of a nuptial event or as a wedding gift, individual prints made from this original watercolor are extremely popular items with Moss collectors.

From the collection of the P. Buckley Moss Museum.

**WINTER'S RUN, Watercolor,
14⅛" x 20¹⁄₁₆", 1986**

*A friendly narrative painting which includes
many Valley-Style elements and references—a
Moss vision of the on-going story of the simple
life viewed within a tradition of integrity.*

This piece presents a number of
iconographic allusions including, of course,
a Mennonite buggy; trees up front; a
strategically-placed bridge; a distant and
doorless generic house; and multiple horizon
lines. Even more important, however, is the
peaceful feeling obtained from viewing the
entire scene which the artist has united
through an economic use of golden hues and
critically intersecting lines.

From the collection of the P. Buckley Moss Museum.

CATS GALORE, Watercolor, 9½" x 6¼", 1986
An example of Moss' humor.

While Pat Moss loves cats and her drollery felines hold an important place in her art, in this watercolor the young man seems to have had just about enough of cats. This piece is pure fun…and shows the artist's noticeable enjoyment in using her talent and her symbols to bring a smile to the faces of the viewers of this somewhat lighter piece of art.

From the collection of Christine Coons, Centerville, Iowa.

COBALT, Watercolor, 28½" x 39¼", 1987
The horse as a widely-recognized Moss symbol.

The horses of P. Buckley Moss typically symbolize human passion and sensuality. All the lines of the horse centered in this painting reaffirm the theory.

   Cobalt is a voluptuous mass of C-scrolls richly illuminated in various shades of brown. The thrust of the horse's head and the freedom of its wild mane add to the symbolic effect.

   This is a painting of youth, strength, and sensuality.

From the collection of the P. Buckley Moss Museum.

TINTERN ABBEY, Watercolor, 12½" x 13½", 1988

A Moss painting of a glorious ruin located in the county of Gwent in Wales just north of Bristol, England.

The subject of this piece, Tintern Abbey, is one of the many Cistercian abbeys suppressed during the mid-1530's by order of Henry VIII.

When Pat Moss first saw the old abbey with its magnificent roofless church, it must have been on one of those typically foggy and rainy British days. In this painting based on actual sketches of the scene, the sun seems to be breaking through the fog forming a cross with the ruined church.

Although this is a spiritual/mystical painting, the artist's humor and her sense of honesty inclined her to add a lone black and white cow in front of the church. Not only does this lone bovine give a homey feeling to the painting as well as a sense of scale, it is a reminder that this once proud stone abbey is no longer functioning as such. Time and history have placed it in the midst of what is really only a pasture.

From the collection of the P. Buckley Moss Museum.

Tintern Abbey

HAGI CASTLE, Watercolor, 15¾" x 13½", 1989

A mood-filled watercolor painted in a classic Japanese style.

In Japan in 1989 following the opening of Pat's exhibition at the Metropolitan Museum of Fine Arts in Tokyo, Pat and her husband Malcolm left for a brief vacation in the San'in region at the western end of the main Japanese island of Honshu. San'in, which means "in the shadow of the mountains," is a beautiful feudal city closely linked to the noble Mori family. Near the city are the remains of the Hagi Castle, a Mori family stronghold during the entire Tokugawa Shogunate period of Japanese history. In the mid-nineteenth century at the time of the Meiji Restoration, the castle was willingly dismantled. The Mori loyally supported the emperor.

Both the history and the beauty of San'in impressed Pat Moss. From sketches done at the site, she chose to paint a number of mood-filled watercolors in a Japanese style. *Hagi Castle* depicts the moat-wall of the ruined castle along with some of its overgrown formal gardens. The colors Pat uses in this piece and the moods she creates differ greatly from the colors and moods she creates in her familiar and better known Valley Style.

From the collection of the P. Buckley Moss Museum.

OCEAN, Watercolor, 11" x 14", 1989

A dramatic emphasis on rocks, water, and distant trees, typical of Moss' more naturalistic watercolor style.

Inspired by the Pacific coast of northern California, *Ocean* is far removed from the rolling countryside of the Shenandoah Valley with its Plain People. Using a porthole format, the artist's attention focuses on the immediate drama of nature to the point where viewers can almost smell the salt air and hear the waves crash.

Pat's West Coast style is both academic and realistic. She fully utilizes the transparent attributes of her watercolor medium to achieve natural effects of light through haze-filled air. Her work in this and similar pieces tends to be poetic rather than narrative.

From the collection of the P. Buckley Moss Museum.

EASTERN RIDE, Watercolor, 7½" x 16½", 1989
*An excellent example of a painting by P. Buckley Moss inspired
by a historical structure, in this case the Daniel Harrison House
(ca. 1749) of Dayton, Virginia.*

Both this house and the town in which it's located have
played an important role in the popular art of Pat Moss. As
one of the earliest structures in the middle part of the
Shenandoah Valley of Virginia, the house influenced the
design of many later structures. Its simple lines can be seen
throughout the Valley as well as in many of Pat's paintings.

The town, on the other hand, is a center for the Old
Order Mennonites of the Valley of Virginia. In Dayton, one
can still see these Plain People in their horse-drawn buggies
going about daily life. These people originally inspired Pat
and became for her "living saints" whose lives were to be
represented time and time again in her art.

Eastern Ride memorably restates the artist's continuing
interest in the people and the places of her beloved Valley
of Virginia.

From the collection of the P. Buckley Moss Museum.

FLOWERS, Oil, 23" x 23", 1990
An academic still-life; stylized and contemporary.

Notice the system of contrasts…large against small, black countering pastels, and curves opposing lines.

From the collection of Malcolm Henderson, Mathews, Virginia.

Floral Fantasia

GEESE AT TWILIGHT, Watercolor, 18" x 30¼", 1990
Moss' ever-popular geese depicted against a glowing sunset.

This watercolor contains many Valley Style elements including the pair of geese and the use of multiple horizon lines. Nonetheless, its overall effectiveness is greatly enhanced by its rich colonization. It is a color field piece without the usual non-objectivity of most contemporary color field art.

From a private collection in Texas.

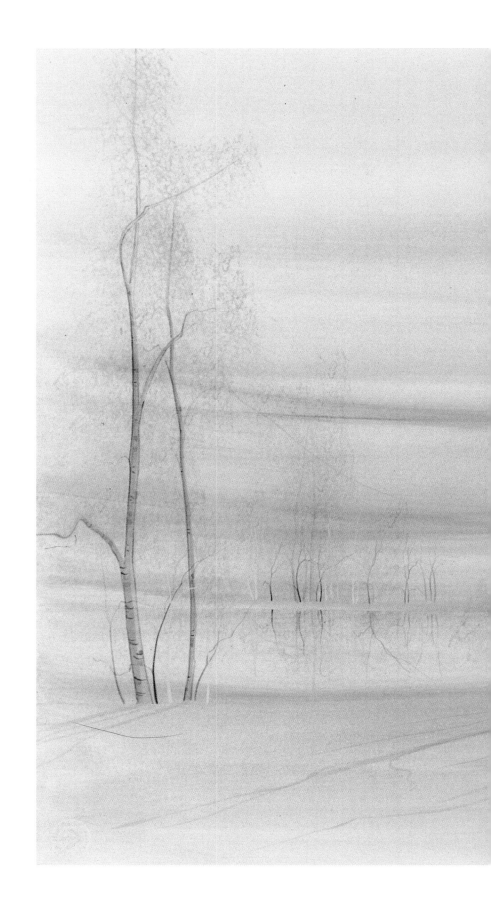

OUR DREAM HOME, Watercolor, 4½" x 17½", 1991
An architectural portrait based on a photograph.

In this piece, Pat captures the mood and warmth of a rustic
log home. This painting pays tribute to the longtime hopes
and dreams fulfilled by its original owners.

From the collection of Mr. and Mrs. Hugh Laverty,

Murrysville, Pennsylvania.

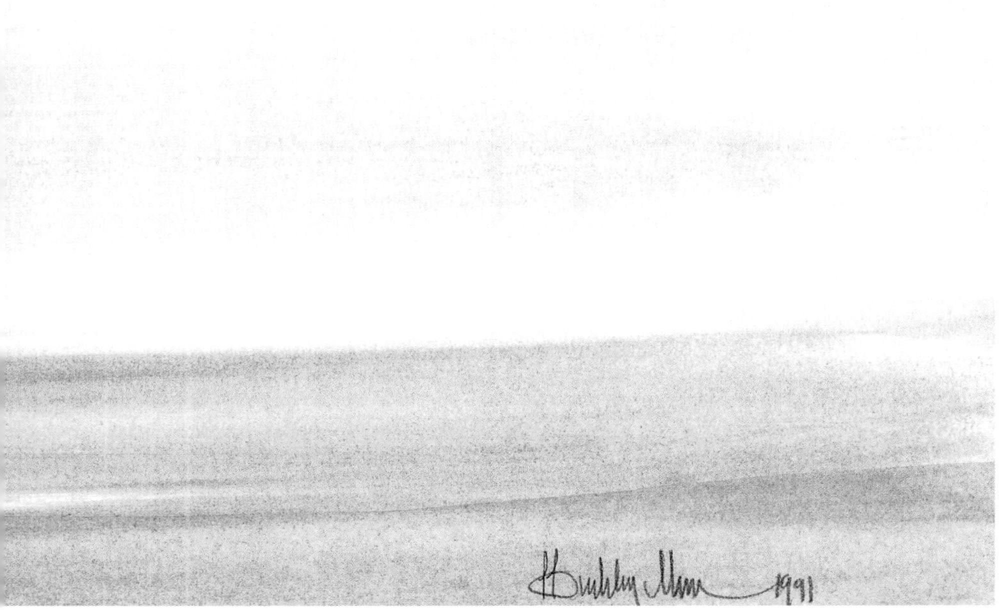

COMMENCEMENT, Watercolor, 15¹⁵⁄₁₆" x 27", 1993
A popular tour-de-force.

Commencement was created for reproduction as a limited-edition offset print to benefit the William and Mary University Alumni Association of Williamsburg, Virginia. It shows an academic procession leaving William and Mary's original 1729/32 college building, Wren Hall. Although students in the procession are not directly represented in the painting, their simplified reflections can be seen in the silver of the College's historic Great Mace carried by the lead female graduate.

From the collection of the P. Buckley Moss Museum.

**SAILBOAT (VALENTINE NUMBER TWO), Watercolor,
5" x 5¼", 1994**
A gift Pat Moss painted for her husband Malcolm.

The inscription on this piece says it all: "To My Love,
Valentine's Day, 1994. Love PB."

From the collection of Malcolm Henderson, Mathews, Virginia.

To my love
Valentines Day 1994

May 94

**SHADOWY RIDE, Watercolor and pastel,
18" x 21¹⁵⁄₁₆", 1995**
A traditional Moss Valley Style painting.

The background of this piece delicately blends blue to green
to gray watercolors with emphatic touches of pink and
purple. The color field gains meaning with the addition of
the covered bridge, the Amish buggy, and the birch trees.

From the P. Buckley Moss Galleries, Ltd. inventory.

Shadowy Ride

CHAPTER SIX
Established Charitable Contributions

The Gentle Art of Sharing

For the past decade, Pat Moss and her husband/ manager Malcolm have allotted a significant portion of their time and energy to charitable endeavors. Pat's commercial success as well as her intuitive concern for others forms the basis for the couple's commitment to share their wealth and insight. Their intent is that others might benefit from Pat's example as well as from her experiences as a learning-impaired child.

During the early 1980s when their charitable efforts began in earnest, Pat and Malcolm tended to give assistance wherever and whenever they were called upon by whatever seemed to them to be a worthy cause.

Soon they found themselves involved in one charitable effort after another, often with little direction or connection. The Moss name assisted fund-raising drives for a myriad of charitable endeavors, from children's hospitals to school outreach to Public Television to battered women to drug rehabilitation to homes for poor families to African relief, etc.

Before the advent of the P. Buckley Moss Society, the Moss organization usually helped an organized charity by either issuing a number of specially designated limited edition offset prints to be sold for the benefit of the charity, or by creating a special print,

either specially framed or remarqued, that the charity itself could raffle or auction.

Many thousands of dollars were raised for worthy causes using these simple methods. In the process, Pat shared her name and often her physical presence with the cause, which on occasion might also involve one of her many nationwide authorized P. Buckley Moss dealerships.

Two examples of Pat's charitable activities prior to establishing the Society are her involvement with WVPT, the Public Television Station serving northwestern, western, and central Virginia and northeastern West Virginia; and with The Mennonite Central Committee out of Akron, Pennsylvania. Both relationships continue to this day.

WVPT was Pat's local Public Television Station during her many years in Waynesboro. In 1980, representatives from the station came to her and requested her help in what they viewed as a relatively straightforward one-time fundraising project. They wanted Pat to supply an original image from which the station would print a limited edition of numbered prints (originally intended to be only 151 pieces). These limited editions either would be sold unframed directly to the public for a set price, or framed and auctioned to high bidders during an on-camera fundraising event. All proceeds would go to the station.

According to a 1982 Moss Portfolio Newsletter, Pat agreed to WVPT's proposal because she was "an ardent supporter of public television for the vital role it has in supporting quality in the performing arts." In addition, she was very much aware of its importance to the elderly and the seriously handicapped.

In that regard, WVPT's request seemed reasonable and she agreed—and every year for the past sixteen years has brought out a new limited edition WVPT Moss print.

To date (1997), these prints have earned the public television station in excess of $800,000.

Another of Pat's long-term charitable endeavors has been her dedicated effort to raise money for The Mennonite African Relief Fund through The Mennonite Central Committee.

Family Love (1986) was the title of the first print issued. All proceeds from the sale of this print were

VALLEY FARM, Limited edition (151 plus 25 Artist's Proofs), Offset print, Image size: 15⁷⁄₁₆" x 11" (from an uncut AP), 1980
A print reproduction of an original watercolor.

The copy shown here is an uncut Artist's Proof. Its four-color offset color line is shown on the right of the print. This line, along with all other border markings, would be cut off as the print is prepared for sale and an appropriate paper size agreed upon.

This was the first in a series of prints that Pat allowed to be issued for the benefit of WVPT Public Television. The top portion of the print shows a familiar Moss Valley scene. A generic house, a distant barn, and silhouetted trees and shrubs sit among the numerous sweeping horizontal lines. Pat depicted this cold and restful winter scene entirely in shades of blue and black.

The lower section of the print presents a popular contrast to the more academic upper section. On the lower foreground, the artist includes five Plain children holding hands as they dance in a circle. Their lively action with its vertical emphasis contrasts sharply with the silent winter scene in which they are portrayed.

This fine mechanically-produced print typifies Pat Moss' ability to blend her scholarly theories of art with her desire to produce an art form that everyone should be able to understand.

designated to the Relief Fund. It has since sold out, earning the Fund $100,000. A second print was then issued (1988) called *Quilting Love*. Priced at $200, it will have earned $200,000 for African relief by the time the edition sells out.

As Pat recalls, "*Quilting Love* was inspired during a visit to Akron [Pennsylvania—the home of the Central Mennonite Committee]. We were being shown around the warehouse at the Material Aid Center where relief goods are collected, packaged, and held ready for shipment to the disaster areas.

"In one room I came across twenty or so Amish ladies working on three quilts. They were grouped around the quilts according to age and therefore experience. It seemed there were great-grannies, grannies, and young mothers. It was such a happy room, with much talk and laughter and exchanging of news between these wives of farmers.

"The Amish may not have telephones with which to pass the time of day with neighbors, but there is certainly something to be said in favor of this direct way of keeping in touch, especially when the end result is a beautiful quilt that will be sold at auction with the proceeds going to the disaster fund."

In 1986, the P. Buckley Moss Society was formally organized, largely through the efforts of its first president, Anne Harbison. Although it began as a small group of Moss admirers who were interested in creating a collectors' club, the Society has grown over the years into a service organization able to help Pat and Malcolm in all phases of their work with charities.

While Pat and Malcolm were never enthralled with the idea of a fan club, Malcolm saw early-on the Society's potential to act as a focusing and screening organization that could separate valid requests for assistance from those that didn't fit into Moss' parameters for charitable giving.

At the present time (1997), the P. Buckley Moss Society claims more than 20,000 members across the entire nation. It publishes an excellent newsletter edited from its beginning by Marlyn DeWaard. An active board of directors, operating currently under President Noreen Newman Johnson, has input into all of Moss' charitable activities.

In addition, the board has recently devised and created the P. Buckley Moss Children's Charities, Ltd. as a tax-exempt not-for-profit entity.

Children's Charities, with its own nascent board under a founding chairman and temporary president Al Wells, has recently hired a director charged to carry out a growing number of nationally significant projects involving children's causes, especially those pertaining to dyslexia and other learning difficulties.

The P. Buckley Moss Society and its offspring, Children's Charities, is headquartered in Waynesboro, Virginia, where it operates under the leadership of the current full-time executive director, Mary Ann Guerrieri.

To further assist the work of the Society, many of its members are consolidated into chapters. These chapters tend to be located in smaller cities and towns all across "the world of Moss," concentrated in the states of Virginia, West Virginia, New York, Ohio, Michigan, Indiana, Illinois, Iowa, Nebraska, Minnesota, Missouri, and Oregon. These chapters represent Moss' charitable

THE MOSS QUILT,
Watercolor, 8⅝" x 14½",
1993
An unofficial P. Buckley Moss Society painting with each square on the quilt representing a Society Chapter located in the United States.

Pat painted this piece to show her pride in and approval of the charity work being accomplished by many of the chapters of the P. Buckley Moss Society.
By 1993, when this original piece was issued as a limited edition offset print, the Moss Society had grown to more than 15,000 members.

interests on a community level and often involve local businesses in their projects through their natural connection to Moss' many widespread authorized dealerships.

One illustration of a contemporary well-focused Moss charity engendered by the Society is the ACT Program (Adults and Children Together). This Society-sponsored program is designed to place mature adults both in learning and play situations with children who have learning or disciplinary problems. Encouraged by Society chapters and often staffed by Society volunteers, ACT programs are now carried out in schools throughout the country.

Today, Pat Moss' usual involvement with a charity begins when the artist and her husband are encouraged to take up a cause recommended by the Moss Society's Board of Directors, a single Moss Society chapter, or perhaps even an individual member.

Raffles remain the fund-raising means-of-choice, with the Moss company providing Society headquarters with an inventory of valuable Moss prints and some original paintings that can be used for this purpose. The Society provides appropriate publicity and often some volunteers to help the actual charitable agency with the projects. These projects usually remain entirely within the domain and under the legal umbrella of the not-for-profit charity.

Finally, the actual raffle, auction, or event occurs, or a special edition of offset prints is offered to the public for sale. Throughout the process, the name of Pat Moss is prominently displayed. Perhaps she and Malcolm undertake some direct promotional activities. Social obligations for the artist and her husband such as a benefit ball, a celebrity luncheon or dinner, or a special Moss speech are often part of the production.

BLUE FLEDGLING, Watercolor, 7⅛" x 4", 1977
A lone baby bird on a bare branch with its beak up and open is one of Pat's
familiar symbols.

For many years, Pat has used this image of a forlorn fledgling as a symbol of
youth and innocence. She likes to show this image to children and say "open
your mouth and sing your own song" as a way to initiate the idea of
creativity and dedicated self-expression.
    In Pat's own life, she seems to see herself as an ugly little bird who did
sing a new song and consequently grew up to be "The People's Artist."

Pat's popular image is both used and enhanced in a process that raises money for worthy charities, a process which involves thousands of volunteers and spreads awareness of critical problems and situations as it promotes the ever-expanding work and the reputation of the Moss Society.

Pat says, "It is wonderful that through the Society I am able to reach out and help so many people and organizations. It is a great encouragement to know that when I give a piece of my work to charity, its marketing will be handled well. My work with charities and schools is the spiritual reward of my career and I treasure it most dearly."

While the P. Buckley Moss Society has become the primary non-profit organization working on Pat's behalf in communities across the United States, Pat Moss' work with schools persists as her own unique and personal project.

Here there can be no substitutes as far as Pat and her young listeners are concerned. Pat herself must share with her kids her own story of educational frustration and near-failure.

In the person of this famous and popular artist, young people perceive an example for their own escape from failure and academic boredom.

Pat Moss, despite her worldly successes, persists in thinking of herself as "that unfortunate and stupid little girl who would never be able to get anything right." Feelings of failure remain for Pat Moss an important psychological factor. It motivates her to share with others a difficult childhood experience while placing herself as a viable adult role model. She understands children's fears and frustrations because she has successfully overcome those same types of fears and frustrations. Consequently, by expressing herself in this way, she cements her own adult personality by calming some of her own inner doubts. Thus, for Pat Moss Henderson, charity is true catharsis.

Fortunately, her husband Malcolm understands Pat's need to reach out to and stand up for kids. He encourages her to use her experiences in the most positive way—especially with school children and in public speaking to both teachers and parents. As a result, for the past twenty years or more, Pat Moss has gone into classrooms and school auditoriums to interact with young audiences. Malcolm Henderson doesn't "think there's anything mystical in Pat's ability to speak out to young people. She was a dyslexic child, and also a rebel growing up with an older sister who did everything right." According to Malcolm, Pat's talent

results naturally from her own experiences as a dyslexic child.

In a teaching/speaking situation, Pat easily responds to young people with an air of self-assurance, an abundance of rhetorical witticisms, and an encouraging series of personal recollections. Her students come to like her as an honest person who cares about them even before they know her as an artist.

Only after a spirit of familiarity has been established will Pat finally ask her young audiences to join her in a spontaneous art project which usually begins with Pat doing a series of simple caricatures. Later on, Pat might supervise a mural drawing with the whole class.

Pat Moss describes a recent encounter with a typical group of troubled young people: "In Davenport, Iowa, we were at a home for girls who had been sexually abused. These kids were about 13 to 17 in age, and they felt like the most unloved things in the whole world.

Now, if you had been dyslexic and people who didn't know what it was called you stupid and dumb and stubborn and impossible.... If you had been stuck with all those things when you were a child, and you walk into a room full of sexually abused children, you look at their faces and think, 'My God, how am I going to lift them?' These girls really felt bad about themselves, and when we got through, we felt as though we had encouraged them, that we had made them feel a little better about themselves.

"You know, I told them that I was a dummy, that people had called me dummy all the time. And I said, 'You know, for a dummy I'm not bad off.' "

To Patricia Buckley Moss, this victory over an unavoidable circumstance falls into the same category as being able to successfully overcome any of life's various inequalities. Hers has been a search for fairness and understanding under conditions that were neither fair nor understood.

The following sentiments are direct quotes from Pat Moss, collected over the past five years from published reports of her schoolroom presentations. They illustrate her philosophy and, more deeply, they indicate the inner motivations for all her art. They document Pat's words, actions, benevolence, and paintings as parts of the same expression and need—the urge to share.

"It's important for every person to feel self-worth...

"Sometimes I still feel like that stupid dumb kid because I didn't have the support you kids have...from mistakes can come good things.

"We do a lot of charity work. It gives us such a good feeling to do it..., special editions sold for charity..., at a dinner the first release of *Davis County Courthouse* was put on sale. Two hundred of these prints were sold at the dinner which netted the fund $20,000....

"You can do anything you want. But the big trick is, choose what you do best and do it. For me, it's drawing. For you, it might be basketball or auto repair or nursing. No matter what it is, if you're doing what you like to do, it's fun. What matters is believing you can do something special with your life.

"Work really hard with that little bit of talent you've got, because people who make it are not the ones who have all the talent; they're the ones who make the most of what they have. It's also really important to like yourself. You have to accept what you're good at and what you're not good at. You have to believe in your own ideas. There are lots of places for all of us in the world. And everything you do, remember to sign it. That means it's yours and nobody else's."

Pat Moss is by nature a person who wants to share—her experience, her philosophy, and her success. Malcolm Henderson, in addition to being generous, is an organizer who understands the diplomacy of giving. Together, they're a team: a successful example of how to share, when and when not to give, and what to expect so as to measure the success of a specific project. Pat is benevolent, Malcolm is perceptive, and the Society helps to focus and accomplish their shared vision.

CHAPTER SEVEN

Honors and Recognitions

The Enduring Phenomenon

Ultimately, Pat's success, her popularity, her charitable giving, and her willingness to become personally involved with learning-impaired young people are the intuitive outgrowths of her own boundless artistic drive as well as her optimistic philosophy.

Without question, Moss has become an appreciated humanitarian and a recognized popular artist. Over the years she has received numerous awards and testimonials. A modest recipient, Pat has said that she has difficulty accepting the facts and kudos of her success. That same old little voice from her past always seems to say, "Can it really be me, or has somebody made a BIG mistake?"

Regardless, one award that she mentions in her autobiography stands above all the rest: The Archbishop Fulton J. Sheen Angel Award presented to her by the Catholic Bishop of St. Petersburg, Florida.

Pat wrote, "The Angel Award is given to a person in media who makes outstanding contributions to public understanding of the God-given worth of the human person. That I, who more than forty years ago became a disciple of Fulton Sheen because of his television message, should now be receiving this award is a tribute to his teachings."

On May 12, 1996, Pat Moss was awarded her third honorary doctorate, not a bad academic record for somebody who was once considered dumb and stupid! The honorary Doctorate of Humane Letters was bestowed on the artist-philanthropist by Bridgewater College of Bridgewater, Virginia (the two earlier degrees had come from Centenary College in New Jersey and Akron University in Ohio). Dr. Phillip C. Stone, President of the College, wrote Pat a letter that sums up many of the aspects of her life. He wrote: "We are thrilled that we have this opportunity to honor you for the extraordinary life that you live. As a parent, artist, community activist, and supporter of so many charitable activities, your life is a good illustration of the balanced and holistic education we promote at Bridgewater College.

"We refuse to define education so narrowly as to include only academic achievement. It is important to us that our students become balanced, fulfilled, and aware of the needs of others. I cannot imagine anyone personifying these attributes better than you. In addition, we are deeply grateful for the many kindnesses you have extended to us in connection with our special education activities and for the thoughtful friendship you extended to our graduating class. We

will enjoy having you as an alumna of Bridgewater College!"

The many distinguished honors that recently have come Pat's way, as well as her ever-increasing work-load, could tend to separate the artist from loyal collectors and demanding public. Starting about 1988, Malcolm encouraged Pat to begin cutting-back on her public-appearance schedule in order for her to devote more time to painting—her first love. About the same time, Malcolm envisioned and created an avenue that allowed P. Buckley Moss to be more conveniently and even more efficiently experienced and shared by her public: the Moss Conventions.

As Pat describes it, "Over the past few years, I have spent a great deal of time traveling to make personal appearances at exhibitions, in part to support the galleries but also to interact with collectors. As a means to cut back on travel time, Malcolm introduced the concept of the Moss Conventions at which collectors and dealers come together on a weekend for various seminars and talks relating to my life and my work. Everyone seems to enjoy the Conventions, particularly my mother, who takes a turn on the stage to talk about my childhood and our family. Since she has no script, I always wonder just what she is going to say!"

To date (1997), sixteen Moss Conventions have been held. The first, on May 20-22, 1988, in Columbus, Ohio, attracted approximately 2,000 people and was a huge success. In The Moss Portfolio Newsletter Malcolm explained the four-fold purpose of the Conventions:

1. To give collectors a chance to meet Pat in a social setting and over a longer period than they would at a gallery show.
2. To provide a forum for lectures and discussions on matters relating to collecting Pat's work.
3. To reduce Pat's travel time by centralizing and consolidating her shows.
4. To allow more Moss dealers a chance to participate in a Moss event.

To date, the Conventions have been held in Ohio, Pennsylvania, Illinois, Georgia, Indiana, Iowa, and Virginia.

THE MUSEUM IN WAYNESBORO, Etching, Image size: 5" x 11³/₄", 1991 A popular Moss rendition of the Museum.

Although Pat has included the P. Buckley Moss Museum in her popular paintings, this dignified yet friendly depiction remains a favorite. While the Museum is essentially a newly constructed building (1988/89), this etching captures the essence of traditional nineteenth-century vernacular Shenendoah Valley architecture..

Perhaps the most impressive vehicle for sharing Pat with a wider audience is the P. Buckley Moss Museum located in Waynesboro, Virginia. The Museum was designed and built expressly to exhibit, preserve, and document Pat's art.

Simultaneously, the Museum presents some of the dynamics of Pat Moss' life and times. This supporting material, along with some of the best examples of Pat's art, blend into a formal tour.

This tour, either with a guide, through labels, or by using a self-guided handbook, serves as a comfortable and enjoyable reintroduction to the entire concept of art and what is actually involved in becoming, being, and remaining a recognized and successful visual artist.

From its beginning, the Moss Museum has been a combination of educational, entertaining, and commercial components. It's situated in a handsome Moravian-style building located on the outskirts of Waynesboro at 150 P. Buckley Moss Drive. The Museum's address on its own city street is a tribute to Pat from the City of Waynesboro and the result of much hard work with the City and Commonwealth by one of Pat's early supporters, educator and later City Councilman Shirly Kiger.

The Museum caters to a primarily transient audience. Though a majority of its visitors are unfamiliar with the serious world of art criticism, they seem to want and appreciate the involvement, the beauty, and the understanding that the subject of art

OPENING CEREMONIES, photograph, May 10, 1989
At the new P. Buckley Moss Museum, Virginia's senior Senator, John
Warner, addresses a VIP audience gathered in the main gallery.

Other speakers, *left to right:* Peter Rippe, Museum Director; Jerry
Gwaltney, Waynesboro's City Manager; Pat Moss; Dr. Thomas
Gorsuch, Waynesboro's Mayor; and Charles Bloom. (Malcolm
Henderson is standing behind the speaker.)

has consistently promised but, in many cases or so it seems, failed to deliver. Often, these people cannot verbalize their craving, their innate hunger for art, but the Moss Museum has been designed to be a friendly place that understands.

May 10, 1989, the opening day for the Museum, was one of great public fanfare. Virginia's senior Senator, John Warner, was the featured speaker. Various civic dignitaries and hundreds of Moss admirers attended the ceremony in the P. Buckley Moss Museum's main gallery.

In his remarks, Senator Warner spoke of Pat as an example of someone who was able to succeed despite learning difficulties. Other speakers praised her for remembering her roots in Waynesboro and thanked Pat for presenting her hometown with such a handsome museum. Pat's art was extolled and guests poured through the museum: it was truly a day for celebration.

It was also a day to test the theory that art, well-presented, with a critical and scholarly interpretation, without any commercial hype, could by itself educate and impress to a point where visitors would actually go into the shop located on the museum's lower floor and purchase reproduction and original prints.

Although the commercial motive has never been the moving force in the Moss Museum's existence (or the primary force in the life of any genuine museum), this vote of confidence engendered by such a generous public reaction was as rewarding in the beginning of the Museum's existence as it is now in the Museum's established day-to-day existence.

The ground-level main floor of the Museum is entirely devoted to exhibitions. Here, visitors are greeted and offered a guided tour encompassing approximately forty years of Moss art with numerous references to what it means to be a leading woman artist in the late twentieth century.

Though tours are built around the art and ideas of P. Buckley Moss and relate her life's story, they also introduce people to the broadest possible range of aesthetic theory and thought. These tours are designed

to help people rediscover art—art in general and Moss art in particular—in new and exciting ways.

The Museum's upper floor, which is also open to the public, houses additional educational exhibitions, a lecture hall and small video theatre, and administrative offices. A computerized registration system tracks as many examples of Moss' art as can be gathered and entered. To date, between 4,000 to 5,000 original paintings by P. Buckley Moss are recorded in the computer's memory. Owners of Moss paintings are encouraged to have their pieces entered into this system so Pat Moss can be the best-documented artist in the entire history of art.

The Moss Museum is open daily. Admission is free and guided tours are always available.

A strong philosophical basis underlies much of what is presented at the Moss Museum. This basis is closely related to the essential aim of most of Pat's art. The Museum predicates its existence on the following:

1. Art is not a science, it does not have to show everything, be consistent, be physically true, or be obviously useful. It doesn't even have to be rationally attractive, though Pat's art usually finds favor with a majority of people.

2. Art is humanity, categorized with other branches of learning (philosophy, languages, history, etc.) that are intended to investigate human constructs and concerns. Pat's art is all of the above.

3. Art, at its best— especially as expressed through the work of Moss—is the free expression of ideas whose

LOVERS, Oil on canvas,
60" x 39", 1990
An oil-wash painting on a
primed canvas depicting in
black lines the heads and
shoulders of a male and a
female form. This highly
romantic and impressionistic
vision reminds one of some
of Modigliani's best work.

The two figures, the lovers,
unite into one flowering
shape that seems to emerge
from an almost cloud-like
blue, maroon, pink, and
white background. They
look out of the work at the
viewer with a sense of calm
and knowing.

This academic piece
combines Pat's love of cyma
lines with her early interest in
color-field painting. Yet,
unlike her earlier non-
objective pieces, the
objective sentiments of this
painting are obvious.

"Lovers" is about love,
when two people become
one united entity. In fact, it's
a celebration of love!

meanings are open to individual interpretation and selected appreciation. At its worst, art can be manipulative, socially injurious, and pedantic.

The Moss Museum presents the art of P. Buckley Moss as an art of celebration. It stands in contrast to much in contemporary art that pertains to alienation and disaffection—art that has scrutinized the underpinnings of society and found them wanting.

Irrespective of the merits of aesthetic affirmation or negation, or as some critics imply—Moss versus a majority of the modernists, the fact remains that when we find ourselves face to face with a legitimate work-of-art, we are in the presence of critical judgement and moral evaluation.

Moss' art is about all of life's more attractive aspects. Pat has judged and evaluated and finds life to be basically good.

Ultimate goodness is the cardinal focus of all of Pat's art. Also, it is the basic tenet of her philosophy, a tenet embraced by members of the P. Buckley Moss Society, by Moss Convention participants, by the staff of the P. Buckley Moss Museum, as well as by the great majority of visitors, and of course, by the thousands of collectors worldwide who treasure their own Moss originals and limited-edition prints.

In the end, however, any verbal description or even a thoughtful analysis is a compromise. Art lives as art, not as words and verbal concepts. This reality is especially true of the art of P. Buckley Moss which seems to automatically elicit love and memory in the heart and soul. A word-filled explanation of this art is merely an erudite exercise.

To rediscover art through the work of P. Buckley Moss means looking at her art and thinking about that which one sees and feels.

Words can illuminate Pat as the true artist she is, but it's the art itself that says, "Here is a disciplined and academic artist with the phenomenal ability to elicit some of human-kind's most fundamental and amiable emotional responses."

Pat summarizes, "In my paintings, I invariably paint the upside of life. I am dedicated to painting the hope of the future—hopes that will seed positive thoughts of love, family, and the beauty of our world."

SOURCES FOR FURTHER REFERENCE:

The P. Buckley Moss Museum
150 P. Buckley Moss Drive
Waynesboro, Virginia 22980-9406
800/343-8643

The Moss Portfolio
1 Poplar Grove Lane
Mathews, Virginia 23109
800/430-1320

The P. Buckley Moss Society
601 Shenandoah Village Drive, Box 1C
Waynesboro, Virginia 22980
540/943-5678

HONORS AND RECOGNITIONS

Patricia Buckley Moss has received many honors and recognitions, including the following.

1976: First Place, National Arts & Crafts Exhibit, Washington, D.C.

1984: Commendation from the House and the Senate of the Commonwealth of Virginia

1985: Roanoke Museum of Fine Arts Retrospective Exhibition

1985: Indianapolis Children's Museum Exhibition

1986: American Artist of the Year, International Wildlife/Western and Americana Show, Chicago

1986: Honorary Doctorate of Fine Art, Centenary College, New Jersey

1986: Cultural Laureate of the Commonwealth of Virginia

1986/1991: International Plate Awards: 1986—"Wedding Joy"; 1987—"The Christening";
        1989—"Hello Grandma"; 1990—"The Wedding"; 1991—"Tender Hands"

1987: New Mammography Unit at Warren Memorial Hospital (Virginia) named the P. Buckley Moss Ward

1987: "Honorary Tar Heel," awarded by the Governor of North Carolina

1988: Commendation from the Senate of the Commonwealth of Pennsylvania

1988: Commendation from the House of Representatives of the State of Michigan

1988: "Sagamore of the Wabash Award," presented by the Governor of Indiana

1988: Contributor of the Year Award, Straight (a non-profit organization), Tampa Bay

1988: Conferred title of Special Honorary Citizen of Takamatsu, Japan

1989: The Nittany Lion Award, Penn State University

1989: "Honorary Kentucky Colonel," appointed by the Governor of Kentucky

1989: Sight-Saving Chairman for The Virginia Affiliate of the National Society to Prevent Blindness

1989: Autobiography Published

1990: Archbishop Fulton J. Sheen Angel Award, Diocese of St. Petersburg, Florida

EASTER AT THE WHITE HOUSE,
photograph, 1995
P. Buckley Moss has been the
designated Easter at the White House
Poster Artist for several years.

Pat and Malcolm Henderson with
President William Clinton and First Lady
Hilary Rodham Clinton.

1990: Metropolitan Museum One Person Exhibition, Tokyo, Japan

1990: Humanitarian of the Year Award, presented at the annual convention of the
Learning Disabilities Association of Indiana

1991: Citation, White House Points of Light Office

1991: "Woman of the Year," awarded by the Gamma Sigma Sigma National Service Sorority

1992: Citation from First Lady, Barbara Bush, recognizing Moss' contributions to learning disabled children

1992: PBS documentary "Split the Wind" about P. Buckley Moss and her art

1993: Learning Disabilities Association of America documentary video, "A Picture of Success"

1993: Honorary Doctor of Humane Letters, University of Akron, Akron, Ohio

1994: Designated Easter at the White House Program artist

1995: Designated Easter at the White House Poster Artist

1995: Included in Carrie Chapman Catt Plaza of Heroines at Iowa State University:

> "P. Buckley Moss, The People's Artist. Through her peaceful artistry we see life as it should be. Through her philanthropic contribution to the welfare of children we see a model to emulate. We honor Pat for her significant contribution to make our world a better place."

1995: Outstanding Dyslexic Calendar Person, JUNE, Learning Disabilities Association (LDA)

1995: Kermezaar Keynote Artist and October Arts Festival Honoree, El Paso, Texas

1996: Honorary Doctor of Humane Letters, Bridgewater College, Bridgewater, Virginia

1996: Distinguished Virginian Award, Virginia Association of Broadcasters

1996: Keynote Speaker for Rotary International, The Homestead, Hot Springs, Virginia

1997: Living Artist Exhibition, March/September, Staten Island Institute of Arts & Sciences

1997: Cooper Union Presidential Citation for Outstanding Entrepreneurship and Advancement of Art

INDEX TO PLATES